AIA Guide
to the
Minneapolis
Lake District

Publication of the

AIA Guide to the Minneapolis Lake District

has been made possible

through generous gifts from

AIA Minnesota

A Society of The American Institute of Architects

John R. Camp

George A. MacPherson Fund

Elmer L. and Eleanor Andersen Fund

Bean Family Fund for Business History

North Star Fund of the Minnesota Historical Society

Larry Millett

AIA Guide to the Minneapolis Lake District

Minnesota Historical Society Press

www.mhspress.org

The Minnesota Historical Society Press is a member of the
Association of American University Presses.

Manufactured in Canada.

10 9 8 7 6 5 4 3 2 1

♾ The paper used in this publication meets the minimum require-
ments of the American National Standard for Information Sciences—
Permanence for Printed Library Materials, ANSI Z39.48-1984.

International Standard Book Number
ISBN 13: 978-0-87351-645-7 (paper)
ISBN 10: 0-87351-645-1 (paper)

Library of Congress Cataloging-in-Publication Data
Millett, Larry, 1947–
    AIA guide to the Minneapolis Lake District / Larry Millett.
      p.   cm.
Includes bibliographical references and index.
    ISBN-13: 978-0-87351-645-7 (pbk. : alk. paper)
    ISBN-10: 0-87351-645-1 (pbk. : alk. paper)
  1. Architecture—Minnesota—Minneapolis—Guidebooks.
  2. Minneapolis (Minn.)—Buildings, structures, etc.—Guidebooks.
  3. Minneapolis (Minn.)—Guidebooks.
  I. Title.

NA735.M5M52   2009
720.9776'579—dc22

                          2008050843

Contents

Symbols Used in this Guidebook

!   A building or place of exceptional architectural and/or historical significance

N   Individually listed on the National Register of Historic Places or included within a National Register Historic District

L   Locally designated as a historic property or within a local historic district

i   A property in which all or part of the interior is included within local historic designation

Abbreviations Used for Select Architectural Firms

ESG Architects	Elness, Swenson Graham Architects
HGA	Hammel, Green and Abrahamson
KKE Architects	Korsunsky Krank Erickson Architects
MS&R Architects	Meyer, Scherer and Rockcastle Architects

Author's Note: This book is a revised, updated, and slightly expanded version of the chapters devoted to the Minneapolis Lake District in my *AIA Guide to the Twin Cities,* published in 2007. Some entries here appear exactly as they are in that book; others have been changed to reflect new information or to provide additional historic background. I have also added a number of entries for buildings that either were omitted from the *AIA Guide* because of space limitations or have been built since its publication.

Locator map: Minneapolis Lake District

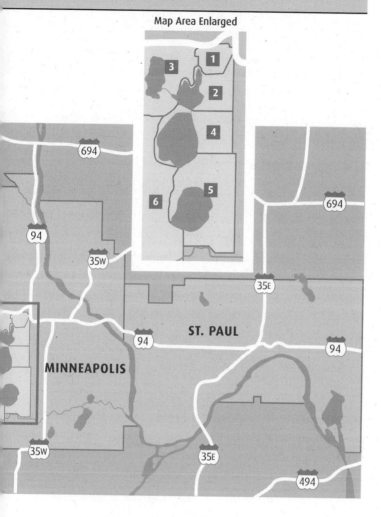

1 Lowry Hill
2 Lake of the Isles and Lowry Hill East
3 Kenwood, Cedar-Isles, and Cedar Lake
4 Lake Calhoun and Uptown
5 Lake Harriet, East Harriet, and Lynnhurst
6 Linden Hills and Fulton

AIA Guide to the Minneapolis Lake District

Overview

The Lake District is Minneapolis's signature neighborhood, a magical meeting of land and water unlike any other in the United States. Five lakes—Harriet, Calhoun, Isles, Cedar, and Brownie—form a chain here, encircled by parks and parkways. By one estimate, more than 5.5 million people a year visit the lakes to walk, jog, bike, skate, swim, or simply enjoy the scenery. Around this glacial gift of water lies a world of sumptuous homes, manicured lawns, and gracious curving streets. This part of the city has been prime residential territory for at least a century and shows no signs of losing its popularity. In recent years, scores of new homes, some of steroidal proportions, have appeared on the district's few open lots or risen from the ruins of "teardowns." Everybody, it seems, wants to live by the lakes.

Although the district has no formal boundaries and takes in all or part of two officially designated neighborhoods (Southwest and Calhoun-Isles), it can be described as the area extending from Interstate 394 on the north to Minnehaha Creek on the south and from Lyndale Avenue on the east to the city limits on the west. Within this eight or so square miles, you'll find a variety of terrains, ranging from standard Minneapolis flat to surprisingly steep hills. The houses and apartments that populate this charmed landscape aren't uniformly elegant, but a general rule of thumb applies: the closer a home is to the water, the larger and more lavish it's likely to be.

Settlement here began well before the city itself was founded. In 1829 Indian agent Lawrence Taliaferro established a village at the southeast corner of Lake Calhoun on the present site of Lakewood Cemetery. Originally known as Cloud Man's Village after the local Dakota chief, it was later renamed Eatonville in honor of a U.S. secretary of war. Missionary brothers Samuel and Gideon Pond were also early arrivals, building a cabin near Lake Calhoun in 1834. A year later, Reverend Jedediah Stevens established a mission at Lake Harriet. These tiny settlements, all located on the Fort Snelling military reservation, soon vanished, largely because of continuing warfare between the Dakota and the Ojibwe.

Even after the military land was opened for settlement in 1855, it took a while for development around the lakes to begin in earnest. The man who more than any other led the way was Colonel (a self-imposed title) William King. Newspaperman, land speculator, visionary, and, judging by his financial adventures, something of a slick operator, King had by 1870 amassed 1,400 acres on the eastern side of Lake Calhoun as well as large holdings around Lake Harriet. He also helped found Lakewood Cemetery, the city's most elegant burial ground, in 1871.

Within a few years, King established the expansive Lyndale Farms, at what is today 38th Street and Bryant Avenue South, built a grand pavilion on the shore of Lake Calhoun, and promptly went bankrupt, though he later reclaimed much of his fortune. He also donated Lake Harriet and surrounding land to the Minneapolis Park Board in 1885, his most extraordinary legacy. Kings Highway, a portion of Dupont Avenue South, is named after him.

Other early entrepreneurs built resort hotels such as the long-vanished Oak Grove House on Cedar Lake, but for the most part the lakes remained pristine until public transportation made them accessible to the masses. By the late 1870s, a horsecar line ran on Lyndale Avenue, while a steam-powered railroad (the so-called Motor Line) operated along Hennepin to Lake Calhoun and then on to Lake Harriet. The Wedge neighborhood between Lyndale and Hennepin saw some of the district's earliest housing, as did Lowry Hill, a prominent glacial ridge near downtown. The introduction of electric streetcar service in 1890 quickened the pace of development, especially in the Kenwood neighborhood, where many pre-1900 homes survive.

The lakes themselves, strewn along an old channel of the Mississippi River, are products of both nature and human engineering. In their natural state, the lakes had marshy shorelines that were prime breeding grounds for mosquitoes and other pests. As a result, only a few homes, most qualifying as country estates, were built near the lakes in the city's early years. The spark needed to ignite development came in the 1880s, when the newly formed Minneapolis Park Board began acquiring land around and between the lakes. Over the next thirty or so years, the board dredged the lakes and used the fill to stabilize their shorelines. Lake of the Isles received an especially thorough makeover and today bears little resemblance to its original appearance. The board also built parkways around Harriet, Calhoun, Isles, and part of Cedar Lake. Later, it dug canals to connect all the lakes except Harriet, a project completed in 1917. Only after these "improvements" did the lakes begin to attract wealthy home builders.

Although it's primarily residential, the Lake District includes one of the city's most important commercial hubs—the ultratrendy (by Minneapolis standards) Uptown area, centered around the intersection of Lake Street and Hennepin Avenue. The district is also home to one of the city's most important cultural institutions, the Walker Art Center (1971 and later), located on a pivotal site at Hennepin and Lyndale, where downtown meets the northern flank of Lowry Hill.

Architecturally, the Lake District is quite diverse. It includes several outstanding religious buildings, among them the Scottish Rite Temple (1894 and later) and Harry Jones's Byzantine-inspired Lakewood Cemetery Memorial Chapel (1910). There's also a notable synagogue, Temple Israel (1928), designed by Liebenberg and Kaplan, a firm best known for its movie theaters, two of which, the Suburban World (1928) and the Uptown (1939), can be found nearby. The district's most beloved public building is the delightful Lake Harriet Band Shell and Refectory (1986) by Bentz/Thompson/Rietow Architects.

For most architectural tourists, however, the Lake District's star attraction is its superb stock of houses. Especially significant are the dozen homes here designed in the early twentieth century by William Purcell, in most cases with his partner, George Elmslie. Their most renowned work, the Purcell-Cutts House (1913), stands a block from Lake of the Isles and is now owned by the Minneapolis Institute of Arts. The two architects were prominent members of the so-called Prairie School founded by Frank Lloyd Wright, and the Lake District can boast of more high-style Prairie houses than anywhere else in the country except for the Chicago suburb of Oak Park, where Wright practiced for many years.

Another sometime member of the Prairie School, Chicago architect George Maher designed the handsome Charles and Helen Winton House (1910) on Lowry Hill. But it wasn't until midcentury that Wright himself secured a commission in the Lake District. The Henry and Frieda Neils House (1951) on Cedar Lake is a late but lovely work from the master and one of only two homes he designed in Minneapolis.

Many other superb houses are scattered throughout the district, including the Franklin Long House (1894, now Groveland Gallery), a sterling example of the Richardsonian Romanesque style; the Lester and Josephine Brooks House (1905) on Lowry Hill; the very peculiar and all but hidden Robert and Isabella Giles House (1908) in the Linden Hills neighborhood; the Spanish-themed Franklin Groves House (1928) overlooking Lake Harriet; and the William Goodfellow House (now the Bakken Library and Museum), a Tudor Revival fantasy from 1930 on Lake Calhoun.

The modern era is also well represented. The Benjamin Gingold House (1958) is a fine example of midcentury design, while the James Stageberg House (1981) offers an exuberant version of postmodernism. More recent homes of note include the Kenneth and Judy Dayton House (1997) on the north side of Lake of the Isles and the James Pohlad House (2008) on Lake Calhoun.

1 Lowry Hill

Lowry Hill

The elevation known as Lowry Hill was once called the Devil's Back-bone, a fanciful name often applied to steep-sided ridges. Unlike Old Nick's presumably gnarled spine, the hill originally came with two crests, which were leveled out in the 1880s as homes began blossoming here. Because of its height and its proximity to the city's lakes as well as to downtown, the hill was identified early on as a prime spot for mansion building, and it remains among the city's choicest residential precincts.

Lowry Hill was the first portion of the Lake District to be platted. Soon-to-be transit kingpin Thomas Lowry, a lawyer who'd arrived in Minneapolis in 1867, was among the real estate men who prepared the plat in 1872. Two years later, Lowry built the first mansion on the hill, which later took his name. But it wasn't until the booming 1880s that other homes began to appear along Mount Curve—Minneapolis's version of St. Paul's Summit Avenue—and other scenic winding streets atop the hill. Many of the grandest houses were built by the city's flour barons, including William Dunwoody and Charles Martin. The grid-iron of streets along the southern reaches of the hill also saw extensive development between about 1890 and 1910. The homes here are generally a bit more modest than those on the crest above.

Today, mansions still line Mount Curve and other streets in Lowry Hill. Quite a few are early- to mid-twentieth-century replacements of Victorian-era homes. More recently, infill properties—mainly condominiums—have been shoehorned into just about every available lot in the neighborhood. Many of these infills are overtly modernist homes that, for the most part, fit quite nicely into the hill's historic environment.

While most of Lowry Hill is residential, its northern edge is dominated by the Walker Art Center, which built its first museum on the site in 1927 after its founder, Thomas Walker, acquired the Lowry mansion. In 1963 the Guthrie Theater also located here, next to the Walker, but Ralph Rapson's seminal building is now gone.

1 Walker Art Center and Minneapolis Sculpture Garden !

1750 Hennepin Ave.

Edward Larrabee Barnes (New York), 1971 and later / addition, Herzog and de Meuron (Switzerland) with HGA, 2005 / sculpture garden, Edward Larrabee Barnes, 1988 / addition to garden (planned), Desvigne-Dalnoky (France)

The Walker and its adjoining sculpture garden occupy a crucial transition point where downtown merges into the hilly terrain of the Lake District. Loring Park, three large churches, and two interstate highways converge here, as do Hennepin and Lyndale Aves. The Walker stands in the middle of it all as a vibrant and highly visible emblem of modernism—in both its art and its architecture.

The evolution of the Walker began when lumberman, entrepreneur, and art collector Thomas Walker bought the old Lowry mansion. Walker immediately began to lay plans for a building to house his art. Located next to his home, the museum building was completed in 1927. It eventually proved too small and was replaced in 1971 by the purple brick building that now forms the northern half of the Walker complex.

The 1971 building is the work of Edward Larrabee Barnes, who studied under such Bauhaus luminaries as Walter Gropius and Marcel Breuer, and it's very much in the minimalist mode of high modernism. Organized into carefully proportioned volumes,

Walker Art Center

Minneapolis Sculpture Garden

the building has always seemed like a distant father figure—admirable for its disciplined strength but hard to love. It works well, however. The eight original galleries pinwheel around a central core, each a half level above or below the next, allowing museumgoers to follow a clear path from one gallery to another.

In 2005, a 130,000-square-foot addition opened to the south along Hennepin Ave., and it's different in almost every conceivable way from Barnes's formal, solemn building. Designed by the Swiss architectural duo of Jacques Herzog and Pierre de Meuron, the irregularly shaped addition is a playful lump of a building perforated with odd-shaped windows and clad in embossed aluminum mesh panels. Wags have had their fun with the addition, likening it to everything from an ice cube to a crumpled cardboard box. The addition—which includes a new entrance lobby, galleries, a museum shop, a restaurant, a 365-seat theater, offices, and underground parking—has experienced its share of problems. It ran well over the construction budget and came with acoustic flaws that required fixing. There have also been complaints about its meandering plan, which is designed to offer you choices, as though you've wandered into a small village with crooked streets. The addition could have used more color—

its exterior beige panels are the approximate shade of dirty snow, not an ideal hue for the long winter months—and it's also less than thrilling when viewed from the rear atop Lowry Hill. Yet for all its imperfections, the addition is great fun, a sort of architectural exploratorium where wonder and surprise are part of the design strategy. It's the kind of building, in other words, that will set you to thinking about the possibilities of architecture, and that alone makes it a must-see work.

The Walker's other key component is the 11-acre Minneapolis Sculpture Garden, which opened in 1988 and was built in cooperation with the Minneapolis Park and Recreation Board. Most visitors, of course, are interested in the garden's extraordinary collection of sculpture, the signature piece being Claes Oldenburg and Coosje van Bruggen's *Spoonbridge and Cherry.* Yet the underlying architecture is equally good. Barnes laid out much of the garden as a grid with wide walkways (or *allées,* as they're called) defined by low walls and hedges. This understated arrangement

Lowry Hill

1   Walker Art Center and Minneapolis
    Sculpture Garden
2   Irene Hixon Whitney Bridge
3   Dunwoody College of Technology
4   The Blake School
5   301 Kenwood Parkway
6   Groveland Gallery
7   Kodet Architectural Group
8   Kenwood Gables Apartments
9   Mount Curve Avenue
10 First Unitarian Society
11 Stanley Partridge House
12 Townhouses
13 A. D. Arundel House
14 Charles J. Martin House
15 Charles and Helen Winton House
16 A. R. Rogers House
17 Lester R. and Josephine Brooks House
18 Louise Foss House
19 John S. Dalrymple House
20 Lawrence S. Donaldson House
21 Condominiums
22 House
23 Houses
24 House
25 House
26 House
27 John Lind House
28 John Dorner House
29 Annie and Elizabeth Quinlan Duplex
30 Pierson-Wold House
31 Sarah H. Knight House
32 George Thompson House
33 House
34 H. R. Williams House
35 E. E. Atkinson House
36 House
37 The Gables Apartments
38 E. G. Wallen House

A   The Bottleneck and the Lowry Hill
    Tunnel
B   Thomas Lowry Park
C   Early twentieth-century houses

L1 Thomas Lowry House, first Walker Art
    Museum, George Daggett House, North
    American Life and Casualty Insurance
    Co. headquarters, Tyrone Guthrie
    Theater, Parade Stadium, Minneapolis
    Armory, Armory Gardens
L2 Plaza Hotel
L3 Franklin B. Long House
L4 George H. Partridge House
L5 Edmund Walton House
L6 William Donaldson House
L7 William and Kate Dunwoody House
L8 Douglas School

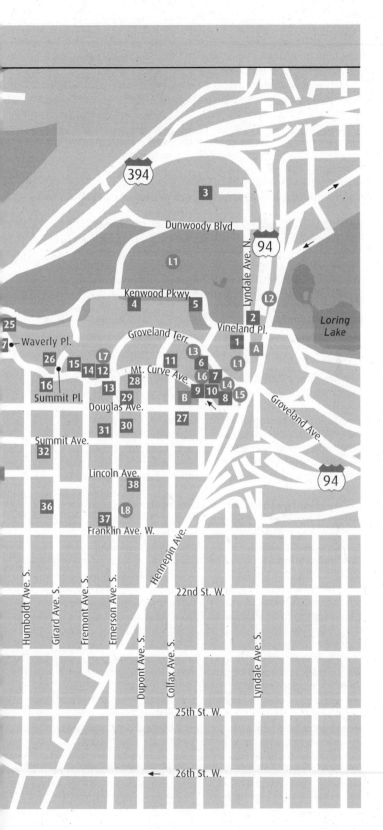

works beautifully, allowing the architecture to serve as a straight man to the art. Barnes also designed the **Sage and John Cowles Conservatory,** the garden's most prominent structure. Plans call for a four-acre addition to the garden to be built on the former site of the Guthrie Theater. As of 2008 the Walker was still trying to raise money for the project, which will be designed by French landscape architect Michel Desvigne.

Lewis S. Gillette House, 1911

Thomas Lowry House, 1925

LOST 1 *Befitting its pivotal location, the site now occupied by the Walker and its sculpture garden has what may well be the most complex building history of any property in Minneapolis. All manner of architectural ghosts haunt the ground here, and while most suffered the usual fate of demolition, at least one—the old Minneapolis Armory—succumbed in a sense to its own weighty presence.*

The architectural history of the site begins in 1874 with the **Thomas Lowry House,** *a French Second Empire–style mansion located about where the 2005 addition to the Walker now stands. The mansion was part of a four-acre estate. After Thomas Walker acquired the property in 1915, he hired the firm of Long and Thorshov to design a museum next to the mansion, which was razed in 1932. Completed in 1927 just before its founder's death, the* **first Walker Art Museum** *was an odd Venetian—Byzantine Revival affair. Later given a slick Moderne makeover, it stood until 1969, when it was torn down to make way for Barnes's new and much larger building.*

Meanwhile, a grand mansion had been built in 1898 along the north side of Groveland Terr. near Bryant Ave. on what is today part

of the Walker's property. The **George Daggett (later Lewis S. Gillette) House,** *at 40 Groveland Terr., was a castellated Tudor Revival fantasy attributed to architects James McLeod and Lowell Lamoreaux. Known as "Eldor Court," the house was purchased in about 1910 by Lewis Gillette, who apparently expanded and remodeled it at about that time, possibly hiring prominent architect Harry Jones for the job. Rising above a series of walls, terraces, and gardens, the house had the appearance of a European baronial estate minus, of course, the peasants. Decorator John Bradstreet was largely responsible for the home's deluxe interiors, which included such wonders as a vast Moorish-style ballroom. It's not clear how long Gillette, an engineer by training who'd made his money in a variety of industrial enterprises, lived in the house. But like many another outsized mansion, the house itself didn't survive into the post–World War II era. It was gone by 1947, when the* **North American Life and Casualty Insurance Co. (later Allianz)** *built a new corporate headquarters on the site. Allianz moved to the suburbs in 2001, and a year later its old building was razed to clear the way for the Walker's addition.*

The most renowned lost building on the Walker site is undoubtedly the **Tyrone Guthrie Theater.** *Designed by Ralph Rapson and completed in 1963, the theater was a high point of architectural modernism in the Twin Cities. Its innovative thrust stage was set in a brilliantly configured auditorium that brought everyone close to the action. Unfortunately, the theater was built on the cheap—the famous screen across the front facade, for example,* was made of plywood—and later "improvements" did away with many of its original features, including the screen. After the Guthrie

Tyrone Guthrie Theater, 1966

announced plans to build a much larger theater complex on the downtown riverfront, preservationists mounted an unsuccessful campaign to save Rapson's building. When the new Guthrie opened in 2006, the old theater was demolished.

The site of the sculpture garden, located directly north of the Walker, also has an interesting history. It's part of the historic Parade Ground, so named because it was once used for military drills. The Minneapolis Park Board began purchasing land here in 1893 and eventually owned 66 acres, much of which was later developed into an athletic complex. In 1951 **Parade Stadium,** seating 17,000 people, was built west of the area now occupied by the sculpture garden. Aquatennial parades began here for years. The stadium was also the site of many high school football games as well as a National Football League game between the Green Bay Packers and the San Francisco Forty-Niners, in September 1951. The stadium was demolished in about 1990 and replaced by multi-use athletic facilities.

Minneapolis Armory, 1910

Although much of the Parade was low and swampy, the city decided that the western portion of it near Lyndale and Hennepin Aves. would be a good place for a new **Minneapolis Armory,** which was duly completed in 1907. Near this massive building, the park board established the **Armory Gardens.** These were designed in accord with the courageous proposition, advanced by parks superintendent Theodore Wirth, that "the Minnesota climate is not so adverse to successful achievement in floriculture as some people from other parts of the country are inclined to believe." The gardens proved to be popular with the public. The armory, on the other hand, proved to be a disaster. It sank into the boggy soil and by 1929 was reported to be in danger of "immediate collapse." Four years later, it was blasted to bits by dynamite, having stood for just 26 years.

POI A The Bottleneck and the Lowry Hill Tunnel

Hennepin Ave., Lyndale Ave., and I-94

1971 (tunnel)

Legend holds that the big turn in Hennepin Ave. between Loring Park and Lowry Hill came about when a farmer insisted that the street be rerouted around a favorite old oak. But the real reason for Hennepin's abrupt change of course has to do more with terrain than trees: the south turn allows Hennepin to take advantage of a natural pass between the glacial ridges that form the hill.

Before Interstate 94 was built, Hennepin crossed Lyndale Ave. here at an impossibly acute angle, producing the infamous "Bottleneck," a traffic free-for-all in which cars, trucks, and trolleys fought it out. Ideally, a freeway would never have been forced through this historic precinct, but there was no stopping highway builders in the 1960s and '70s. The 1,500-foot-long Lowry Hill Tunnel, completed in 1971, does lessen the interstate's impact. Yet with so much surface traffic roaring along Hennepin and Lyndale, it's hard now to gain a sense of how Loring Park once related, visually and by means of connecting streets, to the Parade Grounds and Lowry Hill.

Irene Hixon Whitney Bridge

2 Irene Hixon Whitney Bridge

Over I-94 at Loring Park

Siah Armajani, 1988

A yellow-, blue-, and teal-colored pedestrian and bicycle bridge that crosses the 16 lanes of traffic separating the Walker Art Center and its sculpture garden from Loring Park. Armajani's design mimics both suspension and arch bridges, though in fact it's neither—a bit of artistic license that disturbs engineering purists. Be that as it may, the bridge certainly makes crossing the Hennepin-Lyndale–Interstate 94 traffic barrier a more inviting experience than you'd expect it to be, especially if you take time to read the lovely poem by John Ashbery inscribed on the span's upper beams.

Plaza Hotel, 1908

LOST 2 *The Whitney Bridge crosses the site of the **Plaza Hotel**, which once occupied a wedge of land between Hennepin and Lyndale Aves. at Kenwood Pkwy. Built in 1906 by architect-entrepreneur Walter Keith, the six-story hotel survived until 1960, when clearance began along the route of Interstate 94.*

3 Dunwoody College of Technology

818 Dunwoody Blvd.

Hewitt and Brown, ca. 1917, 1925, and later

A pleasant group of brick buildings with Classical Revival details, especially around the main entrance. Originally known as the Dunwoody Institute and now a two-year technical college, it was founded in 1914 with a $3 million bequest from William H. Dunwoody, then a resident of nearby Lowry Hill.

4 The Blake (Northrop Collegiate) School

511 Kenwood Pkwy.

Hewitt and Brown, 1917; later additions

With its central tower and air of quiet refinement, this Collegiate Gothic–style building is the very image of an upper-crust prep school. It was built for the all-girl Northrop Collegiate School, founded in 1900. Northrop merged with Blake in 1974, and the building now serves as Blake's Upper School.

301 Kenwood Parkway

5 301 Kenwood Parkway

301 Kenwood Pkwy.

ESG Architects, 2003

At a time when an epidemic of nostalgia afflicted most new apartment architecture in the Twin Cities, this mid-rise condominium building came across as a breath of fresh modernist air. Floor-to-ceiling windows alternating with balconies give the building an open feel and also provide residents with views of the Walker Art Center and downtown Minneapolis.

6 Groveland Gallery (Franklin B. Long House) ! *L*

25 Groveland Terr.

Long and Kees, 1894 / addition, 1913

One of the finest houses of any period in Minneapolis, and a superb example of how the Richardsonian Romanesque style could be pared down to produce a bold, sculptural work of architecture almost modern in character. Constructed of rough-faced granite laid up in courses of varying heights, the house is dominated by a steep mountain of a

Groveland Gallery

roof that drops down 30 feet to an inset front porch. Two dormers and a projecting tower with a conical cap provide the only interruptions in the tile roof's precipitous descent. The roof shelters a pair of side gables, which rise above stark walls punctured by irregular window openings. There's not a superfluous gesture anywhere, and the house looks as powerfully convincing today as it did when it was built.

The house's decisive style reflects the personality of its original owner, architect Franklin Long. A partner in one of the city's most successful architectural firms, Long was not a man haunted by doubt. "The longer I live," he once wrote, "the more I am certain that the great difference between men, between the feeble and the powerful . . . is energy, invincible determination, a purpose once fixed, and then death or victory." Spoken like a true Victorian! Long died in 1912, and a year later his house received its only major addition, when the entry porch was extended to the east by enclosing what had originally been a walled terrace. The mansion and its carriage house are now used as an art gallery.

LOST 3 *Before building his new home just a few doors away, architect Franklin Long lived at 41 Groveland Terr. in an 1870s house that he remodeled in 1890 into something quite strange. The **Franklin B.***

Franklin B. Long House, ca. 1895

Long House's *most curious feature was a rounded corner tower that, with its narrow band of second-floor windows, seems to have anticipated the Streamline Moderne style of the 1930s. It's not known when the house came down.*

Kodet Architectural Group

7 Kodet Architectural Group (William S. Nott House) *L*

15 Groveland Terr.

Long and Kees, 1894

Winding along the northern side of Lowry Hill, Groveland Terr. became a favored site for large houses in the 1890s, due in large measure to the efforts of Thomas Lowry. The streetcar magnate, who lived just a stone's throw away, extended one of his lines along nearby Douglas Ave. in 1890 and then replatted the area along Groveland to accommodate mansions. Lowry also commissioned the Minneapolis architectural firm of Long and Kees to design two houses here: this one, purchased by industrialist William Nott, and an even larger mansion (gone) next door for department store owner William Donaldson.

Built of rough-faced stone, the Nott House is especially intriguing because it shows Long and Kees moving away from the Richardsonian Romanesque style, which they'd employed so skillfully for their Minneapolis City Hall (1889–1906), toward a more subdued classical manner. Although this house includes Romanesque details (most notably the porch column capitals), it lacks such familiar features of the style as towers and arched windows. The house has the mixed history typical of near-downtown mansions. After years as a private residence, it was converted to use as a nursing home in 1953. It later took on a third life as offices, and it's now home to an architectural firm.

LOST 4 *A plain two-story building at the southwest corner of Groveland Terr. and Hennepin Ave. occupies the site of the* **George H. Partridge House,** *built in 1897 and expanded in 1904. One of the largest and most sumptuous homes ever built on Lowry Hill, the 25-room Beaux-Arts mansion included a barrel-vaulted ballroom and a five-car garage in which vehicles were parked with the aid of a turntable. The house, which later became home to an institution known as the School of Psychology and Divine Science, was demolished in 1954.*

8 Kenwood Gables Apartments

700 Douglas Ave.

KKE Architects, 1989

At 12 stories, this is the tallest apartment tower in the Lowry Hill neighborhood. It's crowned by several small gables of the type that were affixed like cheap party hats to all manner of buildings during the salad days of postmodernism.

Edmund Walton House, 1894

LOST 5 *This was once the site of the* **Edmund Walton House ("Grey Court"),** *among the loveliest nineteenth-century homes on*

Lowry Hill. *Built in 1893, the house offered a fetching blend of Medieval and Shingle Style elements. It fell to the wrecker in 1959.*

9 Mount Curve Avenue

This winding street at the crest of Lowry Hill is where you'll find the neighborhood's most splendid mansions. As with Summit Ave. in St. Paul, you wish the blufftop side of the street had been preserved as parkland so that the vistas could be readily enjoyed by all. But the lots overlooking downtown were too desirable, and mansions started appearing on this high ground by 1880. A substantial number of these early mansions have been demolished, however, and most of the homes atop the hill today date from the early 1900s and later. The mansions come in virtually all the usual flavors along with some exotic blends, making Mount Curve Ave. one of the best places in the Twin Cities to see the evolution of housing styles through the twentieth century.

POI B Thomas Lowry (Douglas) Park

Douglas and Colfax Aves. South

Minneapolis Park Board, ca. 1919 / renovated, Damon Farber Associates, 1995

An urbane little park with brick paths, a grape arbor, a tumbling watercourse with seven pools, and benches ideal for whiling away time in unproductive fashion.

10 First Unitarian Society

900 Mount Curve Ave.

Roy Thorshov, 1951

An early modernist church in a subdued version of the International Style. A long, covered walkway extends across the front facade, which has windows above the entrance but is otherwise a plain brick box. To the rear, however, ribbons of windows provide views of the city. Overall, the building resembles many elementary schools of this time.

LOST 6 *The rear portion of the Unitarian Society church occupies the site of the* **William Donaldson House,** *which was located at 21 Groveland Terr. between the Nott and Long houses. Like them, it was designed by Long and Kees. Although it was the largest and most elaborately detailed of the trio, the Donaldson House couldn't survive the Great Depression and was razed in 1933.*

11 Stanley Partridge House

1010 Mount Curve Ave.

Harry Jones, 1923

The Tudor Revival style enjoyed great popularity in the early decades of the twentieth century, and there are quite a few examples on Lowry Hill. With its jerkin-roofed gables, angled wings, and unpretentious scale, this brick and stucco house is especially pleasing.

12 Townhouses

1200–22 Mount Curve Ave.

1982

High-rise apartments were proposed for this site in the 1960s after the old Dunwoody mansion was demolished. Neighborhood residents fought such plans for more than a decade, until these low-rise red brick townhomes were finally built. They're quiet and refined, which is undoubtedly what the neighborhood hoped for.

William and Kate Dunwoody House, 1908

LOST 7 *The townhouses were once the site of the* **William and Kate Dunwoody House,** *a brick Tudor Revival mansion built in 1905 to the designs of architect William Channing Whitney. The mansion* was suitably impressive; even better was its beautifully landscaped yard surrounded by balustrades. The house was torn down in 1967.

13 A. D. Arundel House

1203 Mount Curve Ave.

James McLeod, 1895

Set at an angle on its corner lot, this two-story brick house features a curving front portico with wings flaring off to either side. Classical Revival designs tend to be quite staid, but here the architect injected some welcome zip into the proceedings.

Charles J. Martin House

14 Charles J. Martin House N L

1300 Mount Curve Ave.

William Channing Whitney, 1904

One of the better Twin Cities examples of the sort of Beaux-Arts mansion favored by the moneyed crowd in the early twentieth century. Its designer, William Channing Whitney, was the city's premier society architect, and though his work is often a bit dry, he knew how to deliver the luxury goods. Built largely of brick and comfortably ensconced behind a wrought-iron fence, this house is essentially an updated version of a Renaissance palace. It offers a full range of classical paraphernalia: molded window surrounds, dentils, cornices, pediments, quoins, and a balustraded entry porch. Interior features include a monumental staircase, mosaic tile floors, and Italian marble hearths. Much of Lowry Hill is dusted with flour money, and this house is no exception. It was built for Charles Martin, who for many years served as secretary and treasurer of the Washburn Crosby Co., which later evolved into General Mills. Across the street at 1315 Mount Curve is the **J. T. Wyman House** (1909), also in the Renaissance Revival style but more compact and far less ornate than the Martin House.

Charles and Helen Winton House

15 Charles and Helen Winton House ! *L*

1324 Mount Curve Ave.

George Maher, 1910

The only known work in the Twin Cities by George Maher, a Chicago architect who's often lumped in with the Prairie School but whose buildings defy easy categorization. Like many of Maher's houses, this one mixes classical monumentality with details drawn from a variety of sources. The art-glass casement windows, for example, suggest the Prairie Style, although the poppy motif is unique to Maher. The enframed front doorway calls to mind the work of Louis Sullivan, while the pedestal lanterns to either side evoke Viennese Secessionist architecture. The house also features an unusual four-story-high garage and servants' apartment built into the side of the hill. Maher also produced three significant buildings in Winona, MN, including an administrative and manufacturing complex for the Watkins Co. (1911–13), a large summer home known as "Rockledge" (1912, razed in 1987), and the strange, crypto-Egyptian Winona Savings Bank (1911–13). Prone to bouts of depression and never really satisfied that he'd managed to forge his own style, Maher committed suicide in 1926.

16 A. R. Rogers House

1415 Mount Curve Ave.

William Channing Whitney, 1906, 1910

Lowry Hill's very own stone castle, a Tudor Revival estate complete with walls, gates, and a crenellated tower. All that's missing is a moat. The house comes with more than 40 stained-glass windows, five fireplaces, and a ballroom. Included on the property is a carriage house that connects by tunnel to the main house.

Lester R. and Josephine Brooks House

17 Lester R. and Josephine Brooks House !

1600 Mount Curve Ave.

Hewitt and Brown, 1905 and later

The period from 1900 to 1920 produced the most original (and, you could argue, the best) architecture in the history of the Twin Cities. This house is a case in point. Along with the Winton House to the east and the Donaldson House a few doors to the west, it's one of three mansions on Mount Curve that offer a sort of Prairie–Arts and Crafts–Renaissance Revival amalgam. This house's most distinctive feature is a Sullivanesque ornamental frieze that runs the entire length of the front facade beneath the eaves. Plaques of similar design are affixed near the recessed front door, which opens onto a terrace. Above are three windows divided by colonettes and framed by a drip molding that steps down and around the doorway. Architect Edwin Hewitt wasn't of the Prairie persuasion, but he did work in the Arts and Crafts mode, and he pulls off the stylistic mix here with great aplomb. The house was built for Josephine Brooks, whose husband, Lester, had died in 1902.

Lester Brooks was a native of New York State whose family moved to southeastern Minnesota when he was nine. He became president of a flour mill in Winona before moving in 1884 to Minneapolis, where he was involved in banking, lumbering, and milling.

18 Louise Foss House

1606 Mount Curve Ave.

Ernest Kennedy, 1906

An attractive Medieval–Tudor Revival house. It looks older than it is because it's built with walls of local Platteville limestone, a material rarely used for luxury homes after the 1880s.

19 John S. Dalrymple House

1700 Mount Curve Ave.

Bliss and Campbell, 1960

A one-story brick house with high transom windows, exposed roof beams, and a side-entry garage. The house was obviously designed for maximum privacy, so much so that even the front door is hidden from the street.

Lawrence S. Donaldson House

20 Lawrence S. Donaldson House

1712 Mount Curve Ave.

Kees and Colburn, 1907

Lawrence S. Donaldson, who with his brother William founded the department store bearing the family name, built this house just up the hill from William's mansion on Groveland Terr. Constructed largely of brick and exquisitely detailed, the house at first glance appears to be a conventional Renaissance Revival exercise. Look more closely, however, and you'll see the design's

diverse origins. The terra-cotta ornament, as well as the railings on the front terrace, derive their intertwining forms from Louis Sullivan (who was building his famous bank in Owatonna, MN, at the time this house went up). The row of casement windows in the front dormer is more Prairie Style, while the curved porch roof resembles a Beaux-Arts theater marquee. Somehow, it all works.

21 Condominiums

1124–28 Kenwood Pkwy.

Mark Mack (California), 1993–94

Colorful stucco homes topped by barrel-vaulted roofs.

1118 Kenwood Pkwy.

22 House

1118 Kenwood Pkwy.

Mark Mack (California), 2000

A well-detailed stucco house in a style that might be called California Modern. Because it's set on a narrow lot, the house unfolds itself from front to back in a series of irregular volumes that suggest an interesting floor plan within.

23 Houses

903 Kenwood Pkwy.

1993

909 Kenwood Pkwy.

Altus Architecture1Design, 2003

915 Kenwood Pkwy.

1987

A row of three stucco houses wedged into the steep face of Lowry Hill. The designs are interesting enough—especially 909 Kenwood, which uses a large curving element as a kind of shield against nearby Interstate 394—but if you compare this trio to the hefty brick and stone mansions just up the hill on Mount Curve, you get a sense for how lightweight modern construction has become.

1521 Waverly Pl.

24 House

1521 Waverly Pl.

1996

It's not often that you see a house clad in stainless steel, but here it is, sleek and shiny as can be. This stylish house is among many modern infills on Lowry Hill that make no attempt to disguise their modernity, and one of the real pleasures of the neighborhood is the lively architectural interplay between old and new.

1520 Waverly Pl.

25 House

1520 Waverly Pl.

Horty Elving and Associates, 1970

If you substituted brick for this house's wood and metal sheathing and eliminated most of the windows, you'd have a small-scale version of the 1971 Walker Art Center building down the hill. Like the Walker, this house adheres to a cool, severe brand of modernism, with little appeal to the emotions.

26 House

46 Summit Pl.

ca. 1880s?

Wedged in among all the mansions here is this small, considerably altered house—possibly built in the 1880s or earlier—that shows Greek Revival characteristics. It was moved to this site in 1904.

27 John Lind House *L*

1775 Colfax Ave. South

William Channing Whitney, 1905

A red brick Georgian Revival house most notable as the one-time home of John Lind, a Swedish-born lawyer who, running as a Democrat in 1898, became the first non-Republican in 40 years to be elected governor of Minnesota. He also served four terms in the U.S House of Representatives. Described as a dour man, Lind lost his bid for reelection as governor in 1900 and then did something that other politicians can only dream of. After delivering a farewell address to the state legislature, he walked to the offices of the *St. Paul Dispatch*, a frequent critic of his administration, and punched the managing editor in the nose. Those were the days.

28 John Dorner House

1720 Dupont Ave. South

ca. 1900

A Classical Revival house with an unusual porch, its colossal Ionic columns cut into at their mid-points by cross members that feature a diamond motif. These bold horizontals give the facade a distinctly cellular look of the sort you'd associate with something far more modern. It's not clear when the cross members appeared in their present form, but they presumably were once part of a second-story porch with railings.

29 Annie and Elizabeth Quinlan Duplex

1711 Emerson Ave. South

Frederick Ackerman (New York), 1924

This suave Italian Renaissance Revival house might be thought of as architect Frederick Ackerman's trial run for his equally elegant Young Quinlan Building, completed just two years later downtown. Clothier Elizabeth Quinlan, who lived in this duplex

Annie and Elizabeth Quinlan Duplex

with her mother, was the client behind both buildings, and here— as in her store—she opted for a certain kind of understated historicism that, before art deco swept all before it, represented the height of architectural fashion in the 1920s. This stucco house sits like a palazzo in miniature on its large lot just south of Mount Curve, and it's come down through the years with few changes.

30 Pierson-Wold House N

1779 Emerson Ave. South

Theron P. Healy, 1892

The second owner of this brick Colonial Revival house was Theodore T. Wold, a banker. In 1917 his son, Ernest, went off to World War I in France, where he was trained as a pilot with the First Aero Squadron. He was killed in battle in 1918, as was another young Minnesota flyer named Cyrus Chamberlain. The Twin Cities airport was later named Wold-Chamberlain Field in their honor.

31 Sarah H. Knight House

1200 Summit Ave.

Harry Jones, 1910

A charming house that skillfully blends Arts and Crafts and Renaissance Revival motifs. Note how the arches in the entry porch echo those of the wall dormers above. Sarah Harrison Knight, the

wealthy daughter of a pioneering Minneapolis hardware whole-

Sarah H. Knight House

saler, was a friend of Harry Jones and for many years owned a cabin next to his on Lake Minnetonka.

32 George Thompson House

1800 Girard Ave. South

William Kenyon, 1909

An attractive brick and half-timbered house nestled behind a low wall and a protective screen of pines.

1778 James Ave. South

33 House

1778 James Ave. South

1926

One of Lowry Hill's best Period Revival houses. With its gentle undulations, calm lines, and ivied stucco walls, this house has an English Arts and Crafts feel, although the way the roof swirls down over the front door is pure 1920s architectural theater.

34 H. R. Williams House

1728 Logan Ave. South

1898

A nicely detailed Colonial Revival house, though it's hard to see behind all the trees.

35 E. E. Atkinson House

1901 Logan Ave. South

Albert Van Dyck, 1914

A brick Beaux-Arts mansion that would be right at home on Mount

Curve. Note the fine terra-cotta ornament, the elaborate carriage house, and the terrace that looks out over Kenwood Park.

1800 block Irving Ave. South

POI C Early twentieth-century houses

ca. 1750–2100 Irving Ave. South (from Douglas Ave. to 22nd St. West)

various architects, ca. 1895–ca. 1915

Much of southern Lowry Hill was built up in the early 1900s after streetcar service had been extended down Douglas Ave. These four blocks along Irving Ave. offer a representative collection of homes from this period, mostly in one version or another of Classical, Colonial, or Georgian Revival. Among the houses of note are those at 1766 Irving, built in 1901 and featuring a cross-gabled gambrel roof and a semicircular front porch; 1790 Irving, which dates from 1907 and sports a giant Corinthian portico; 1800 Irving, a Queen Anne–Colonial Revival mix from about 1900; and 1937 Irving, which was built in 1901 and has a curving wrap-around porch.

36 House

1912 Girard Ave. South

Bertrand and Keith, 1894

This house's brownstone entry arch is in the Richardsonian Romanesque manner, but other elements fall within the realm of late Queen Anne.

37 The Gables Apartments

1200–1208 Franklin Ave. West

Keith Co., 1908

A Mission Revival–style apartment building with two wings connected by a charming arcaded courtyard.

Douglas School, 1896

LOST 8 *In 1894* ***Douglas School,*** *a handsome Renaissance Revival building, opened where the Lowry Hill Manor Homes, 1921–35 Emerson Ave. South and 1920–52 Dupont Ave. South, now stand. Designed by architect Warren E. Dunnell, the two-story brick school featured a high hip roof and a steep front gable, both of which had been lopped off by the time the building was demolished in the 1970s. Its replacement, an understated townhome complex in stucco and brick, was built by Ben Meyerson in 1976.*

38 E. G. Wallen House

1900 Dupont Ave. South

1896

A rigorously symmetrical Classical Revival house. The semicircular portico is echoed by an arched pediment atop the central dormer.

Lake of the Isles and Lowry Hill East

There are two distinct neighborhoods here, and their differences illustrate the role of water, parks, and mass transportation in molding Minneapolis. The area around Lake of the Isles and immediately to the east is one of the city's residential gold coasts and has been from the time the lake was, in effect, created by dredging around 1910. Before that time, Lake of the Isles was deemed to be little better than a pestilential swamp, and its ragged shores had attracted only half a dozen or so adventuresome home builders. Once the modern lake emerged out of the mire, however, mansions blossomed all around it like luxuriant flowers. Among them was the grandiose but ill-fated Charles Gates Mansion (1913). Today, more than 120 houses, including some of the largest and most expensive in the city, surround the lake, endowing it with an atmosphere of well-heeled serenity.

Just to the east of the lake, extending to Hennepin Avenue, the blocks filled in with slightly smaller houses that are nonetheless of very high quality. There are many excellent Arts and Crafts–era homes here, such as the Arnett Leslie House (1917), as well as two of Purcell and Elmslie's finest works: the Edward L. Powers House (1911) on 26th Street West and the Purcell-Cutts House (1913) on Lake Place.

Farther east, between two busy commercial corridors—Hennepin and Lyndale avenues—you'll find a more varied housing stock in the neighborhood officially known as Lowry Hill East but more commonly referred to as the Wedge. Heavy traffic surges around and through this neighborhood, which has a much more frenetic feel than the area around Lake of the Isles. Because horsecar and later train service along Lyndale began serving this part of the city as early as the 1870s, the Wedge has some Victorian-era houses mixed in with old apartment buildings, new upscale condominiums, and modest working-class homes. Among the most notable historic homes here is the John G. and Minnie Gluek House (1902) on Bryant Avenue South.

POI A Lake of the Isles parks and parkway

Minneapolis Park Board, 1889–93, 1907–11

This lake, with its long northern finger and pair of wooded islands, is essentially a man-made creation. In its pre-engineered state, it was a shallow marsh interspersed with four small islands. Before improvement, the lake and its surroundings consisted of 100 acres of water, 67 acres of swamp, and 33 acres of dry land. By the time dredging operations ended in 1911, there were 120 acres of water and 80 acres of land. The first major reshaping occurred in the early 1880s, when two islands near the south end of the lake were removed to make way for a rail line. Later in the decade, the Minneapolis Park Board acquired the entire lake and its shoreline, then undertook four years of dredging. Completed in 1893, this work stabilized the shoreline so that a parkway could be built. It required yet another bout of dredging, between 1907 and 1911, before the lake took on its present appearance. The Kenilworth Lagoon, through which Isles connects to Cedar Lake, was completed in 1913. All of the fill around the lake inevitably deteriorated over the years, and since 2001 the Minneapolis Park and Recreation Board has spent more than $5 million on a long-term shoreline reclamation project.

The mansions that surround the lake mostly date from between 1900 and 1930, with those along the east shore tending to be a bit older than those on the western side. New houses spring up whenever a site becomes available, and some of these are of high quality as well.

1 George C. Stiles House

2801 Lake of the Isles Pkwy. East

Harry Jones, 1910

At first glance this appears to be a formal Beaux-Arts house, and it's certainly in that territory. But the Egyptian capitals on the porch columns are an odd touch, while the plainness of the overall detailing owes something to the Arts and Crafts sensibility of the time. All in all, a sharp design from the wide-ranging Harry Jones.

George B. Clifford Jr. House

2 George B. Clifford Jr. House

2601 Lake of the Isles Pkwy. East

Ernest Kennedy, 1931

A Tudor Revival house dolled up in stone, stucco, and half-timbering. With its quaint tower and unreal ordering of parts, it could easily do double duty as a set for *Robin Hood* or some other costume romance. The original owner was a son of one of the founders of the Cream of Wheat Co.

A. M. Fiterman House

3 A. M. Fiterman House

2525 Lake of the Isles Pkwy. East

Edwin Lundie, 1953

One of Edwin Lundie's typically elegant houses, in the Cape Cod variant of Colonial Revival. The house, built of brick with a fading coat of white paint that creates a mottled effect, is large and complex in plan. Even so, it looks modest on the outside, where Lundie assembled the volumes in such a way that the house resembles a small village of buildings.

Charles Gates Mansion, 1916

LOST 1 *The houses at 2505 and 2525 Lake of the Isles Pkwy. East occupy the site of what was once the city's largest and costliest house: the* **Charles Gates Mansion.** *The Renaissance Revival–style mansion was built in 1913 for the ill-fated son of John W. ("Bet-a-Million") Gates, a legendary businessman who made a fortune in barbed wire, railroading, and oil, among other enterprises. He acquired his colorful sobriquet after wagering a tidy $1 million on a horse race in England in 1900. Charles G. Gates seems to have inherited his father's flamboyance gene. After marrying Florence Hopwood, Gates announced plans to build a "cottage" overlooking Lake of the Isles. Coming in at 38,000 square feet (larger than James J. Hill's mansion in St. Paul), the house was a stone palace outfitted with the best of everything money could buy, including what is reputed to have been the nation's first home air-conditioning system, installed by Carrier. Unfortunately for Gates, money couldn't buy him a reliable appendix, and he died, apparently of complications from surgery, before his mansion was completed.*

Gates's widow, who must have been considered quite a catch, remarried in 1916 and moved elsewhere. A St. Paul physician, Dr. Dwight Brooks, bought the house but never lived in it. Brooks died in 1929. Once the Great Depression set in, there were no buyers for such a costly property, and the mansion was demolished in 1933. However, much of its deluxe interior was salvaged, including a marble staircase

Lake of the Isles & Lowry Hill East

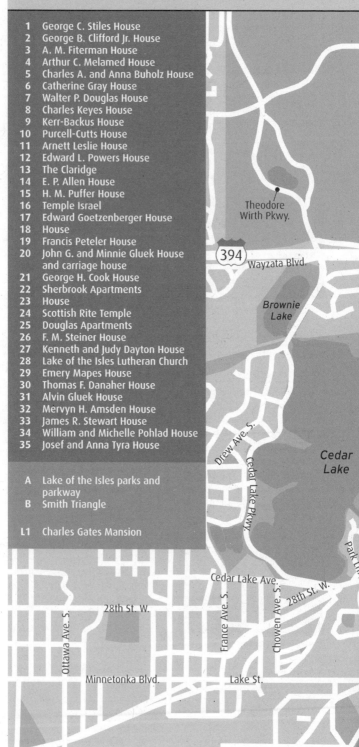

1   George C. Stiles House
2   George B. Clifford Jr. House
3   A. M. Fiterman House
4   Arthur C. Melamed House
5   Charles A. and Anna Buholz House
6   Catherine Gray House
7   Walter P. Douglas House
8   Charles Keyes House
9   Kerr-Backus House
10 Purcell-Cutts House
11 Arnett Leslie House
12 Edward L. Powers House
13 The Claridge
14 E. P. Allen House
15 H. M. Puffer House
16 Temple Israel
17 Edward Goetzenberger House
18 House
19 Francis Peteler House
20 John G. and Minnie Gluek House
    and carriage house
21 George H. Cook House
22 Sherbrook Apartments
23 House
24 Scottish Rite Temple
25 Douglas Apartments
26 F. M. Steiner House
27 Kenneth and Judy Dayton House
28 Lake of the Isles Lutheran Church
29 Emery Mapes House
30 Thomas F. Danaher House
31 Alvin Gluek House
32 Mervyn H. Amsden House
33 James R. Stewart House
34 William and Michelle Pohlad House
35 Josef and Anna Tyra House

A   Lake of the Isles parks and
    parkway
B   Smith Triangle

L1 Charles Gates Mansion

Lake of the Isles

later installed in the Burbank-Livingston-Griggs House on St. Paul's Summit Ave.

4 Arthur C. Melamed House

2505 Lake of the Isles Pkwy. East

1958

A large, long, modernist house clad in fieldstone—a favorite material of architects in the 1950s. The house looks to have much fine detailing.

Charles A. and Anna Buholz House

5 Charles A. and Anna Buholz House

2427 Lake of the Isles Pkwy. East

Frederick Soper, 1911

Minneapolis's very own Mediterranean villa, and quite a showstopper. Mounted on a high corner lot above a series of gates, staircases, walls, and terraces, the L-shaped house is coated in gleaming white stucco and includes a spectacular curving veranda that poses prettily beneath a fanlike pergola. Not much is known about architect Frederick Soper, who seems to have practiced in Kansas City, MO, before moving north.

Catherine Gray House

6 Catherine Gray House

2409 Lake of the Isles Pkwy. East

Purcell and Feick, 1908 / additions, 1918 and later

This house was one of William Purcell's first projects in Minneapolis, done before George Elmslie became his partner (though Elmslie helped with the design). Purcell began planning the house for himself but later named it for his grandmother, who came from Chicago in 1907 to live with him. As built, the house was heavily influenced by Frank Lloyd Wright's "Fireproof Home for $5,000," a design published in 1907. Prairie Style features here include high brick corner piers, a shallow hipped roof, and bands of casement windows, some of which wrap around corners. Originally, the house had a one-story entry pavilion on its north side, where there's now an addition. In 2004, Minnesota Public Radio acquired the house from a longtime supporter, refurbished it, and sold it for more than $1.5 million as part of a fundraising campaign.

7 Walter P. Douglas House

2405 Lake of the Isles Pkwy. East

Francis W. Fitzpatrick (Duluth), 1887

Built before the first round of dredging started in 1889, this house is among the oldest on the lake. It's an extensively renovated Queen Anne–Shingle mix.

8 Charles Keyes House *L*

2225 Lake of the Isles Pkwy. East

Adam Lansing Dorr, 1904

An Arts and Crafts foursquare in which Victorian vestiges, such as a polygonal bay above the porch, still linger. The house's first owner was a lawyer who became active in civic affairs and ran unsuccessfully for mayor of Minneapolis in 1935.

9 Kerr-Backus House

2201 Lake of the Isles Pkwy. East

1911 / Kenyon and Maine, 1922

One of the lake's most picturesque houses, set on a large lot behind a stone and iron fence complete with arched gateways. The stuccoed house, entered via an arcade off 22nd St. West, is a Mediterranean–Medieval English blend and a good example of the mix-and-match historicism common in the 1920s. The house's original owner, M. B. Kerr, was a sales manager at Munsingwear,

Kerr-Backus House

Inc. The second owner, who commissioned a large makeover of the property in 1922, was Edward W. Backus. A lumberman and paper milling magnate, Backus made and lost a fortune in the north woods. The small northern Minnesota town of Backus is named after him.

Purcell-Cutts House

10 Purcell-Cutts House ! N Ʒ

2328 Lake Pl.

Purcell and Elmslie, 1913 / restored and renovated, MacDonald and Mack Architects, 1990

In 1911, three years after his marriage to Edna Summy, William Purcell began to think about creating a new house for his family, which included a recently adopted infant son. Although Purcell's partnership with George Elmslie had produced few lucrative commissions, he had family money and so was able to spend $14,000, a goodly sum at the time, to build this exquisite house just a block from Lake of the Isles. Purcell's aim was to create a progressive house for what he called "modern American family life" (which in his case later included divorce). The result was this Prairie Style masterpiece.

Dubbed by Elmslie as "the Little Joker," the house isn't especially large, but it's gorgeously

designed down to the last detail. In few other houses of its size will you find so many architectural ideas carried out with such great verve. Set well back on its lot to catch views of the lake, the house from the outside presents a series of rectilinear volumes, one of which juts out toward the sidewalk and ends in an array of tall art-glass windows. Rows of smaller art-glass windows flow

Purcell-Cutts House interior

across the second story, where stencil patterns in the stucco walls create a frieze of sorts beneath an extremely low-pitched roof. The main entry is off to one side beneath an inset porch. Here you'll find a projecting beam that culminates in a swirl of Elmslie's characteristic sawn-wood ornament as well as stained-glass windows adorned with this message: "Peek a Boo."

Within, the house commands an intricate array of spaces on five levels. At the heart of the design is a spatial procession that extends along an axis from a sunken living room in front, up half a level to a dining room with a prowlike projection, and then out to a screened rear porch. A common tent ceiling unifies the living and dining rooms, which open to an entry hall on a level midway between them. The upstairs includes two bedrooms, the largest of which can be subdivided by screens.

Although the floor plan is ingenious, what sets this house apart is the quality of its details. The best Prairie houses combine sleek modern lines with ornament of dazzling beauty and inventiveness. No other modern style except for art deco (rarely used for houses) has matched this synthesis. Here, Elmslie's gifts as an ornamentalist are fully evident, in art-glass windows, stencilwork, desks and chairs, light fixtures, and other furnishings. The living room fireplace is particularly fine. Gold- and glass-flecked mortar glitters between the hearth's long Roman bricks while, above, a mural by artist Charles Livingston Bull emerges from a framework of wood strips that forms an elegant arch.

Purcell and his family did not stay in the house for long. Lacking commissions, the firm of Purcell and Elmslie was all but defunct by 1918, when Purcell moved from Minneapolis and put the house up for sale. It was purchased by Anson Cutts, Sr., a railroad traffic manager, and his wife, Edna, a singer who gave private concerts at the house. The couple's only son, Anson Cutts, Jr.—a painter, writer, and critic—moved back to the house in the 1960s to care for his ailing mother. Upon his death in 1985, he bequeathed the house to the Minneapolis Institute of Arts, which undertook an extensive restoration. In 1990 the house, occupied by art institute staff, was opened to limited public tours, and it remains one of the glories of the city.

Arnett Leslie House

11 Arnett Leslie House

2424 Lake Pl.

Long, Lamoreaux and Long, 1917

Purcell and Elmslie are Minneapolis's best-known Prairie architects, but other local firms tried

their hand at progressive design, sometimes with more than passable results. This L-shaped house lacks the dynamism of Purcell's own home, but it's still nicely done, with a centralized formal entry and broadly proportioned windows that derive from the work of George Maher. The first owner was president of the Leslie Paper Co. and in 1930 cofounded the Ampersand Club, an organization devoted to fine printing and the book arts that remains active today.

Edward L. Powers House

12 Edward L. Powers House !

1635 26th St. West

Purcell Feick and Elmslie, 1911

Although not as well known as the Purcell-Cutts House two blocks away, this home is of comparable quality. Clad in stucco above brick, it has an unusual plan in which the living room is at the rear of the house so as to capture what were once good views of Lake of the Isles. To accommodate this unorthodox layout, the main entry is well back to one side. The house's two-story polygonal front bay echoes a semicircular bay off the living room, a feature the architects also employed at their Decker House (1912, razed) at Lake Minnetonka.

This home is among the most richly adorned of Purcell and Elmslie's residential works, despite the fact that they had to do some major redesigning to cut costs. Elmslie had just joined the firm when the commission came in, and he poured out a wealth of gorgeous ornament in sawn wood, stencils, glass, and terra-cotta, including a magnificent plaque over the main fireplace.

Edward L. Powers was a vice president of the Butler Brothers Co., which a few years earlier had constructed a superb warehouse designed by Harry Jones in downtown Minneapolis. Perhaps Powers's familiarity with that building sharpened his appetite for good architecture, which is certainly what he got here. In any event, Purcell described Powers and his wife as "people of fine intelligence and very appreciative of our methods and results." He also wrote, years later, that "this Powers House is a distinguished piece of work, and it still stands fresh and interesting, truly contemporary with the most thoughtful buildings of today." Purcell wasn't always a reliable guide to his own architecture, but in this case it would be hard to disagree with him.

13 The Claridge

2519 Humboldt Ave. South

Alexander Rose, 1922

This ivy-covered, center-court apartment building is not extraordinary for its time, yet it achieves a kind of dignified elegance that seems beyond the reach of even the most upscale modern condominiums. A key difference, of course, is the materials. This brick building looks as though it was made to last, whereas many modern apartments look as though they were made to amortize over 20 years, and not a day longer.

14 E. P. Allen House

2425 Humboldt Ave. South

1914

One of the nicest of the neighborhood's Mission Revival houses. A triple-arched porch dominates the design.

15 H. M. Puffer House

1414 24th St. West

Dorr and Dorr, 1911

A bungalow placed on a corner lot so that its broad side serves as the front. The composition of the three gables gives the house a restful, gracious quality.

Temple Israel

16 Temple Israel

2324 Emerson Ave. South

*Liebenberg and Kaplan, 1928 / addition, **Rabbi Max Shapiro Education Building**, 1955 / addition, Bentz/Thompson/Rietow Architects, 1987*

Initially known as Shaarai Tov (Gates of Goodness) and organized in 1878, this is the oldest Jewish congregation in Minneapolis. The congregation, which became Temple Israel in 1920, occupied several other buildings before constructing this Classical Revival–style synagogue. Symbolic elements are worked into the design, including the five front doors that represent the books of the Torah. The sanctuary is renowned for its acoustics. Architect Jack Liebenberg used tiles made from sugar beet stalks to modulate the sound. The tiles worked so well here that he also used them in his theaters, including the nearby Suburban World. The Rabbi Max Shapiro Education Building was added to the synagogue in 1955, and another addition completed in 1987 includes a small theater, meeting rooms, and offices.

POI B Smith Triangle

24th St. West and Hennepin Ave. / Art: Thomas Lowry Monument (bronze and stone sculptures), Karl Bitter, 1915

This monument to streetcar tycoon Thomas Lowry was originally at the south end of the "Bottleneck" at Lyndale and Hennepin Aves. Construction of Interstate 94 drastically altered the intersection, and the monument—which consists of a bronze statue of Lowry set before a stone wall with carved figures—was moved here in about 1970.

Edward Goetzenberger House

17 Edward Goetzenberger House

2621 Emerson Ave. South

Purcell and Feick, 1910

One of Purcell's early pre-Elmslie designs. The house, which appears to be in excellent condition, is a two-story box with a gable roof and a rather crowded arrangement of windows around the front door. Goetzenberger was a sheet metal worker who'd become acquainted with Purcell while employed on an earlier project.

18 House

2701 Dupont Ave. South

1884

An attractive Shingle Style house with front and side gables and interesting carved paneling above one of the doors. The porch doesn't look to be original.

19 Francis Peteler House

2726 Dupont Ave. South

1887 / remodeled, ca. 1920s

This house has a Spanish Revival stucco facade, but it was originally Italianate, as evidenced by the vestigial cupola on the roof. The man who built the house, Francis Peteler, invented a railroad dump car that brought him a tidy fortune.

20 John G. and Minnie Gluek House and carriage house N L

2447 Bryant Ave. South

house, William Kenyon, 1902 / carriage house, Boehme and Cordella, 1902

This isn't the largest or most "correct" Georgian Revival house in Minneapolis, but it may just be the most beautiful. Occupying three city lots, it was built for a son of Gottlieb Gluek, who founded the Minneapolis brewery that bore his name. The house, sheathed entirely in white clapboard, includes a balustraded front porch that extends northward to form a porte cochere.

John G. and Minnie Gluek House

Architect William Kenyon took great care in composing the major elevations, which offer Palladian windows, elegant split pediments, and other fine details. One example: the south gable (facing 25th St.) terminates in a small triangular window—a feature that cannot have had any practical use but that adds a wonderful grace note to the design. Equal care was lavished on the carriage house, which for some reason the Glueks hired the firm of Boehme and Cordella, rather than Kenyon, to design. John Gluek and his wife, Minnie, enjoyed their house for only a few years. He was an early automobile enthusiast, and in 1908 they were killed when their car struck a train near Lake Minnetonka.

21 George H. Cook House

2400 Bryant Ave. South

Keith Co., 1902

The 2400 block of Bryant features an array of Colonial Revival houses built between about 1900 and 1910. This house, one of the largest of the group, includes an outsized split pediment above the front porch. Note also the unorthodox oval that hovers over the Palladian window in the front gable.

22 Sherbrook Apartments

2003 Aldrich Ave. South

1923

A standard 1920s brick apartment building with one unusual feature in the form of white pilasters stuck like chunky exclamation points at the corners.

23 House

2121 Colfax Ave. South

ca. 1890

A towered brick Victorian, eclectic in style and somewhat the worse for wear. Its most peculiar feature is a large keystone in the front gable that resembles a giant golf tee.

24 Scottish Rite Temple (Fowler Methodist Episcopal Church) N i

2011 Dupont Ave. South

Warren H. Hayes, 1894 / Harry Jones, 1907 / remodeled, Bertrand and Chamberlin, 1916

Constructed of ultra-hard quartzite from southwestern Minnesota with red sandstone trim, this Romanesque Revival–style building features two massive towers, an arcaded entry porch and a 24-foot-diameter rose window divided into 12 stained-glass "petals." The building has a complicated design history. Warren Hayes was hired by the Fowler Methodist congregation in 1894 to draw plans for the church. By the time of his death in 1899, however, the congregation had raised only enough money to build part of his design—a chapel intended to be at the rear of the church. It wasn't until 1906 that the congregation had the wherewithal to complete the project. Architect Harry Jones was then called in to finish what Hayes had started. Jones followed the general style set by Hayes but also beefed up elements of the original design to create the building you see today.

In 1915 the Fowler congregation merged with Hennepin Avenue Methodist Church and sold this building to the Scottish Rite Temple, a Masonic organization. Although the church's vaulted auditorium was modified a bit in 1916 to accommodate Masonic rituals, it retains many of its original features, including an extensive stained-glass program. In May 1931, what's said to have been the largest funeral in Minneapolis history was held here for local daredevil and stunt pilot Charles "Speed" Holman, who died when his plane crashed during a performance in Omaha, NE.

Scottish Rite Temple

Lake of the Isles

25 Douglas Apartments

2000–2014 Dupont Ave. South

ca. 1900

An urbane trio of Georgian Revival–style apartment buildings with gambrel roofs and two-story porticos.

26 F. M. Steiner House

1720 Franklin Ave. West

Kees and Bolstad, 1926

This staid Renaissance Revival–style home conveys the image of a high-toned clubhouse or perhaps even a library. Few houses of this type were built in the Twin Cities after the Roaring Twenties came to their unhappy end.

Kenneth and Judy Dayton House

27 Kenneth and Judy Dayton House

1719 Franklin Ave. West

Vincent James Associates and Hargreaves Associates (landscape architects), 1997 / Art: glass and sliding panels, James Carpenter Design Associates (New York)

A temple of high modernism executed in teak, stone, glass, and steel. Its owners, from the Dayton's Department Store family, acquired two older houses here near the north end of Lake of the Isles, then tore them down to make way for this home. Set amid precisely landscaped grounds, the house is clad in Indiana limestone with teak framing around the windows, and it's aligned so that the south and west sides face the lake. Its two wings partially enclose a granite-paved motor court and a sculpted lawn, creating the sense of a private compound. The house's floor-to-ceiling windows, chaste detailing, insistent rectilinearity, and aura

of deluxe understatement all call to mind one of Ludwig Mies van der Rohe's modernist pavilions, and you have to believe the old master himself might have approved of the design (though Mies being Mies, he would have quibbled over details). Within, the house includes sliding panels and glass designed by artist James Carpenter.

28 Lake of the Isles Lutheran (Congregational) Church

2020 Lake of the Isles Pkwy. West

Hewitt and Brown, 1928

This handsome English Gothic–style church is the only non-residential building of note overlooking the lake. Constructed of Minnesota limestone and featuring an offset tower, the building was originally home to a Congregational church.

Emery Mapes House

29 Emery Mapes House

2218 Lake of the Isles Pkwy. West

Harry Jones, 1915

Among the biggest mansions on the lake, this brick Renaissance Revival palace includes a splendid second-floor terrace that extends for almost the entire length of the house. It was built on a suitably grand scale for Emery Mapes, a founder of the Cream of Wheat Co. in 1893. Mapes devised advertising campaigns that made the cereal—milled from coarse wheat middlings—into a national brand. Cream of Wheat continued to be made in Minneapolis until 2002.

30 Thomas F. Danaher House

2296 Lake of the Isles Pkwy. West

1910

A trio of steep gables enlivens this picturesque Tudor Revival house, built for a real estate dealer who obviously knew the value of curb appeal.

Alvin Gluek House

31 Alvin Gluek House

2374 Lake of the Isles Pkwy. West

Boehme and Cordella, 1916

A superb Arts and Crafts–style house built for the grandson of the founder of Gluek's Brewery in Minneapolis. The art-glass windows that light the main staircase are especially fine. Alvin Gluek was an innovator in the brewery business and is often credited with developing the first malt liquor—a high-alcohol variation of beer—in 1942.

Mervyn H. Amsden House

32 Mervyn H. Amsden House

2388 Lake of the Isles Pkwy. West

Liebenberg Kaplan and Martin, 1922

A Cotswold Cottage house in full regalia, complete with a wood

shake roof that curls down over the eaves in imitation of thatching. Quite a few houses of this type were built in the 1920s, but this may well be the largest example in Minneapolis. Its scenic qualities are much abetted by a healthy growth of vines.

33 James R. Stewart House

2424 Lake of the Isles Pkwy. West

Carl Gage, 1929

The 1920s English Cottage look boiled down to a kind of pictorial minimalism. What little elaboration there is focuses on the windows, which are framed by brick quoins but are so flat that they almost look as though they were glued onto the stucco walls.

34 William and Michelle Pohlad House

2528 Lake of the Isles Pkwy. West

Altus Architecture+Design, 2009

One of the largest new homes to appear on the lake in many years. This choice lot became available after a 2005 fire destroyed a Beaux-Arts mansion that had occupied the site since the 1920s.

35 Josef and Anna Tyra House

2572 Lake of the Isles Pkwy. West

Harry Jones, 1908

Classical Revival meets Arts and Crafts, with intriguing results. The house was built for an Austrian immigrant who found success in the New World in the roofing and cornice business.

Kenwood, Cedar-Isles, and Cedar Lake

Occupying the hilly ground between Lake of the Isles and Cedar Lake, Kenwood is one of the city's most charming residential enclaves. The neighborhood, which extends north along Kenwood Parkway to the flanks of Lowry Hill, has a reclusive quality, in part because it's buffered on virtually all sides by either water or railroad tracks, many of which now function as biking-hiking trails. Kenwood's winding streets were laid out in 1880, and within a decade more than 30 homes had already been built here. Rail lines spurred initial development, serving commuters from a small station. In 1890 streetcars reached the neighborhood when a line was extended to 21st Street West and Penn Avenue. In addition to its founding stock of Victorians, Kenwood offers houses in the usual variety of styles, ranging from neoclassical to Prairie (including two designed by Purcell and Elmslie) to Period Revival. Among the modern-era infills is Frank Lloyd Wright's beautiful Neils House (1951) on the eastern side of Cedar Lake. However, Kenwood's best-known property is probably the so-called "Mary Tyler Moore" House (1892), the exterior of which was depicted as part of the comedienne's long-running television show.

The Cedar-Isles neighborhood to the south of Kenwood occupies the area between Calhoun and Cedar Lakes. Here, the homes tend to be smaller and newer than those in Kenwood, and there are also quite a few apartments and duplexes, including Dean Court (1982–85), a grain elevator converted to housing.

Although the area to the west and north of Cedar Lake falls within the boundaries of the Bryn Mawr neighborhood, it is very much a part of the Lake District. Here you'll find Brownie Lake, a small gem set deep in a natural bowl at the southern end of Theodore Wirth Park, as well as the western shore of Cedar Lake, which features two wooded peninsulas. The area is heavily residential, and while few of the houses are as grand as those around Lake of the Isles, they're generally very pleasing. This neighborhood can also boast of one major commercial monument—Target Financial Services (1954), located amid 30 green acres just west of Brownie Lake.

1 Kenwood Water Tower *L*

1724 Kenwood Pkwy.

Andrew Rinker and Frederick Cappelen (engineer), 1910

At 110 feet, this octagonal brick water tower, vaguely Medieval in appearance, is Kenwood's tallest structure. In the late 1970s there was a proposal to convert the tower, which hasn't been used to store water since 1954, into condominiums. The scheme failed, however, and the tower is now designated as a local landmark.

1800 Oliver Ave. South

2 Houses

1800, 1804 Oliver Ave. South

D. C. Bennett, 1923

Screened by heavy foliage during the summer months, these two

Kenwood Water Tower

similar but not identical "Mediterranean" houses occupy a hilltop lot and share an unusually elaborate staircase. The steps lead from Oliver in a single wide flight, then divide at a niched wall before continuing up to the houses.

William and Patricia King House

3 William and Patricia King House

1941 Penn Ave. South

Close Associates, 1952

Winton and Elizabeth Close specialized in low-key but very carefully designed houses that strove for a high degree of functionalism. This house, an excellent example of their work, bears some similarity to Frank Lloyd Wright's Usonian homes of the same period.

4 T. E. Byrnes House

1908 Kenwood Pkwy.

Walter J. Keith, ca. 1900

A stone, brick, shingle, and stucco house that merrily combines various Tudor Revival and Arts and Crafts motifs with a sort of French Gothic tower.

5 W. A. Loveland House

1938 Kenwood Pkwy.

1909

A large Arts and Crafts four-square with arched porch windows and a glassy third-floor addition.

6 House

1969 Queen Ave. South

George Bertrand, 1889

A Colonial Revival house with many distinctive touches, including a pair of gambrel-roofed front dormers with windows that bow out ever so slightly.

7 B. R. Coppage House

1912 Queen Ave. South

Harry Jones, 1891

One of Harry Jones's playful, castlelike houses, presided over by a corner tower wearing a splendid witch's-hat roof. Unfortunately, the house has lost its original porch as well as its clapboard siding, now covered by stucco.

S. E. Davis House

8 S. E. Davis ("Mary Tyler Moore") House

2104 Kenwood Pkwy.

Edward S. Stebbins, 1892 / renovated, 2006

A Queen Anne house that became a local icon by virtue of its association with the popular *Mary Tyler Moore Show,* which aired on network television from 1970 to 1977. An exterior shot of the house identified it as the location of Moore's apartment. Had this been true, she would have been living beyond her means as a producer for a bargain-basement television station. The house, extensively renovated in 2006, is in fact a private residence.

9 C. H. Ross House

2000 Kenwood Pkwy.

McLeod and Lamoreaux, 1899

One of Kenwood's delights. The house is a late Victorian take on French Gothic, as evidenced by *fleur-de-lis* adorning the front

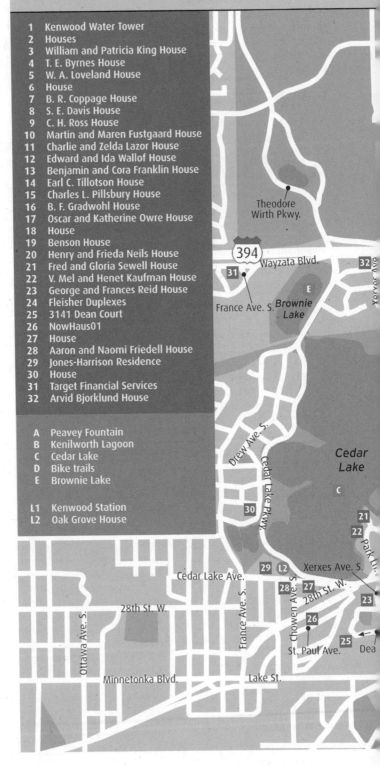

Kenwood, Cedar-Isles, & Cedar Lake

1   Kenwood Water Tower
2   Houses
3   William and Patricia King House
4   T. E. Byrnes House
5   W. A. Loveland House
6   House
7   B. R. Coppage House
8   S. E. Davis House
9   C. H. Ross House
10 Martin and Maren Fustgaard House
11 Charlie and Zelda Lazor House
12 Edward and Ida Wallof House
13 Benjamin and Cora Franklin House
14 Earl C. Tillotson House
15 Charles L. Pillsbury House
16 B. F. Gradwohl House
17 Oscar and Katherine Owre House
18 House
19 Benson House
20 Henry and Frieda Neils House
21 Fred and Gloria Sewell House
22 V. Mel and Henet Kaufman House
23 George and Frances Reid House
24 Fleisher Duplexes
25 3141 Dean Court
26 NowHaus01
27 House
28 Aaron and Naomi Friedell House
29 Jones-Harrison Residence
30 House
31 Target Financial Services
32 Arvid Bjorklund House

A   Peavey Fountain
B   Kenilworth Lagoon
C   Cedar Lake
D   Bike trails
E   Brownie Lake

L1 Kenwood Station
L2 Oak Grove House

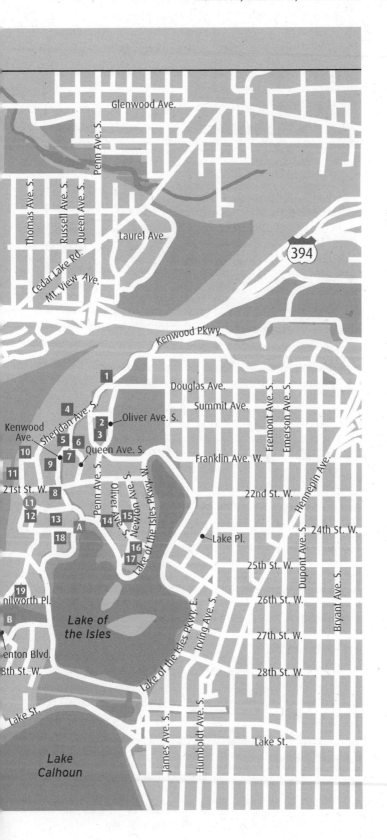

C. H. Ross House

bay, pointed arch windows, and an exceptionally tall, steep roof punctuated by two charming mini-dormers. The large carriage house is equally picturesque.

Martin and Maren Fustgaard House

10 Martin and Maren Fustgaard House

2512 Franklin Ave. West

Martin Fustgaard, 2003

If Prince ever decides to make a sequel to *Purple Rain,* here's just the house he needs. Sporting a color scheme that's heavy on purple, violet, and fuchsia, this whimsical stucco house created a bit of a stir when it went up. One unhappy neighbor was quoted in a newspaper story as saying, "I've got Disneyland across the street." Well, not exactly. The house—a scenic affair with a round tower, a busy roofline, and much whimsical detailing, including a sun, a moon, and a star—is actually rooted in the Storybook Style of the 1920s. That style wasn't Walt Disney's doing, but it did come out of Hollywood, and, indeed, this house does have a kind of coastal exuberance seldom seen in the buttoned-down Midwest. Considering what the likely alternative would have been—a big fat McMansion—it's hard to see how this purple fantasy could do Kenwood any lasting harm.

11 Charlie and Zelda Lazor ("Flatpak") House

2024 Thomas Ave. South

Lazor Office (Charlie Lazor), 2004

Modern architects have long been infatuated with modular and prefabricated housing designed to supplant the standard

Charlie and Zelda Lazor House

American "stick-built" home, which uses a structural system—known as balloon or platform framing—that's now well over 150 years old. From Buckminster Fuller's geodesic domes to Frank Lloyd Wright's Usonians to the all-metal Lustrons built after World War II, these dreams of a sort of house-in-a-kit have never made much headway in the marketplace.

This house, designed by and for Minneapolis architect Charlie Lazor, is one of the latest entries in the modular movement. Its name derives from the fact that it's built largely of wood, steel, and glass panels that can readily be shipped in so-called flat packs. The panels can be combined in different ways to produce a variety of designs. Here, the results are truly elegant, without any of the clunkiness that usually afflicts modular housing. Whether the Flatpak house can find a significant niche in the housing market remains to be seen, but this prototype certainly makes you hope that it will.

12 Edward and Ida Wallof House

2200 Sheridan Ave. South

Harry Jones, 1891 / addition and restoration, David Heide and Mark Nelson, 2006

Among the oldest—and most frequently photographed—

houses in Kenwood. A Queen Anne–Shingle Style mix designed by the prolific Harry Jones, the house includes a sweeping stone porch and a broad shingled arch

Edward and Ida Wallof House

above the Palladian window in the front gable. It was built for Edward G. Wallof and his wife, Ida. Edward, who founded a machine tool company in Minneapolis, lived here with his extended family, including a brother named William. Considered something of a ne'er-do-well, William was nonetheless handy with a camera, and he took scores of photographs of his family as well as many scenes of early life in Kenwood. His photographs can now be found in the collections of the Minneapolis Public Library. A large rear addition completed in 2006 includes a new kitchen and a family room.

LOST 1 *One of William Wallof's photo subjects was* **Kenwood Station,** *located at 21st St. West and Thomas Ave. The small wooden station, which sported a cupola, was built in the 1870s by the Minneapolis and St. Louis Railroad to serve commuters. Streetcars doomed commuter rail service, however, and by the 1890s the station had been converted into a private residence. It was torn down in the 1970s. The* **Hotel Kenwood,** *a three-story wood-frame building, was once at West 21st and Sheridan Ave., just a block from the station. Built in 1896, the hotel was mainly used to house railroad workers. It was torn down in 1928.*

Benjamin and Cora Franklin House

13 Benjamin and Cora Franklin House *L*

2405 22nd St. West

1915

A rare local example of the Viennese Secession style, one of modernism's many early variants. The flat-roofed stucco and brick house consists of a high central block flanked by one-story wings. A veranda leads up to the front door, which is set between large windows with leaded-glass transoms. The wings and the upper portion of the main block feature casement windows separated by thin piers. Decorating each pier is a glazed tile set at the bottom of an inset band of stucco that descends from the eaves—a subtle touch that gives each tile the look of a pendant hung from above (similar tile detailing can be found on a house nearby at 2215 Sheridan Ave. South).

Inside, the Franklin house is organized around a high-ceilinged living room that occupies the central block. It's not known who designed the house, but there's evidence to suggest that it was inspired by at least one similar home produced a few years earlier in California. There's another house of this type in the Lake District, at 2773 Dean Pkwy., built in 1919. Its architect is also unknown.

POI A Peavey Fountain

Kenwood Pkwy. at Lake of the Isles Pkwy. West

1891

A fountain dedicated to dead horses. Frank Peavey gave the fountain to the city in 1891, with the idea that horses could use it to quench their thirst. After World War I, the fountain was rededicated to honor horses from the 151st Field Artillery killed in action.

14 Earl C. Tillotson House

2316 Oliver Ave. South

Purcell Feick and Elmslie, 1912

An obtrusive front porch (which once had a second story as well) mars the appearance of this house, which is among several Purcell and Elmslie designed with high gable roofs. According to Purcell, the house went through the budget wringer a number of times, and it shows. This is not one of the firm's choicer designs.

15 Charles L. Pillsbury House

2216 Newton Ave. South

Carl B. Stravs, 1910

A peculiar house from architect Carl Stravs, who was born in the old Austro-Hungarian Empire and studied in Vienna. Among the curiosities here are dormers with oddly clipped roofs and trapezoidal windows around the front door. The first owner was an electrical engineer by training who later became an executive vice president of Munsingwear, Inc.

16 B. F. Gradwohl House

2621 Newton Ave. South

Albert Van Dyck, 1918

A formal, three-story Renaissance Revival house that makes for an interesting comparison with the Owre house next door. Architect Albert Van Dyck is an obscure figure, but he seems to have designed some of the more lavish houses in this part of the city around the time of World War I.

17 Oscar and Katherine Owre House N L

2625 Newton Ave. South

Purcell Feick and Elmslie, 1912 / restored, MacDonald and Mack Architects, 1996

A disciplined and efficient design from Purcell and Elmslie. The house is essentially a stuccoed cube with a notch in one corner for the front door. Bands of casement windows punch through the smooth walls beneath a low-pitched roof that rises from

Oscar and Katherine Owre House

broad eaves. Extending out from this compact volume are a porch in front and what was originally a maid's room to the rear. Within is one of the firm's characteristic open plans, organized around a fireplace situated between the living and dining rooms. Budget limitations kept ornament to a minimum.

The house was built for Dr. Oscar Owre, a surgeon, and his wife, Katherine. Purcell later wrote, "Oscar was scared to death that his building was going to cost him more than he could afford, and had been told by all his friends that every building operation carried on by an architect was loaded with heartbreaking extras which would spoil all his fun, if not ruin him financially." Purcell managed to assuage the doctor's fears, and the house cost $17,275, which was $35 under budget. Katherine Owre, incidentally, was a daughter of reformer Jacob Riis, whose influential book *How the Other Half Lives* painted a grim picture of New York City's slums.

18 House

2421 Russell Ave. South

1907 / rebuilt, Hugh G. S. Peacock, 1967

An old house turned into a prominent example of the shed-roof style that was imported into the Twin Cities from California in the 1960s and 1970s.

19 Benson House

2700 Kenilworth Pl.

Sarah Susanka, 1994

Architect Sarah Susanka scored a popular hit with her 1998 book *The Not So Big House*. This, by contrast, is a not-so-little house that strives for a sort of Prairie Revival look but comes across as a bland box with lots of windows. Perhaps it was her experience with houses like this that led Susanka to begin thinking that smaller might be better.

POI B Kenilworth Lagoon

Between Lake of the Isles and Cedar Lake

Minneapolis Park Board, 1913

This is the longest of the three canals built between 1911 and 1917 to link four Minneapolis lakes. The water level in Cedar dropped by six feet when this canal opened.

20 Henry and Frieda Neils House ! N L

2801 Burnham Blvd.

Frank Lloyd Wright, 1951

This gorgeous house, one of only two in Minneapolis designed by Frank Lloyd Wright, shows how even an architect as supremely gifted as Wright could benefit from close collaboration with his clients. Wright's talents—a fabulous eye, an uncanny command of scale, an almost mystical feel for materials, and a highly refined spatial sensibility—are all on display here. Yet the house's distinctive marble walls were first suggested by Henry and Frieda Neils, both of whom were exceptionally knowledgeable about architec-

ture and design. At the time the house was built, Henry was the retired president of the Flour City Ornamental Iron Co. in Minneapolis. Frieda was the artistically minded daughter of the iron company's founder and also an enthusiastic admirer of Wright's work.

In 1949 the couple began making plans for a new home overlooking Cedar Lake on property adjoining their existing home, built in 1923, at 2815 Burnham Blvd. Believing Wright could give them just the house they wanted, the couple journeyed to the great architect's Wisconsin estate to meet with him. At some point they showed him a picture of their 1920s "Mediterranean" house. Wright agreed that they needed a new home and suggested—probably facetiously, though you never could tell with him—that they should "burn the old one down."

The Neilses didn't follow that incendiary bit of advice, but they did indeed hire Wright to design their new home, with splendid results. In many ways the house is typical of the so-called Usonian designs that Wright developed in the 1930s. It's L shaped, has just one story (with no basement), uses a limited palette of materials, and is planned in a way that separates what Wright called "active" and "quiet" zones. The house's main "active" area is its living room, which features a 17-foot-high vaulted ceiling and offers views of the lake across a walled terrace. The long wing that extends into a triple carport holds the quiet area, devoted to bedrooms and a gallery connecting to the front door, which in

Henry and Frieda Neils House

typical Wrightian fashion is well hidden.

The house is the only one Wright ever built with marble walls. The colored and textured walls, which taper as they rise, consist of small blocks of "cull" marble left over from other building projects. Henry Neils, who was a trustee of a marble and tile company, had acquired the stone at a good price and convinced Wright to use it. To achieve the effect he desired, Wright had the masons chip away any polished edges before laying up a piece of marble. However, when the walls were finally completed, neither Wright nor his clients liked the overall color. Wright dispatched one of his students to supervise a process by which some blocks were stained to create just the right color effects.

The home's aluminum windows, made by Neils's company, are also unique in Wright's residential work, since he generally preferred wooden frames. Neils's connection to a lumber company owned by his father resulted in another atypical feature: interior paneling made of western larch as opposed to the cypress or redwood Wright usually preferred. In 2008 the house was sold to new owners after being in the Neils family for 57 years.

21 Fred and Gloria Sewell House

16 Park Ln.

Charles R. Stinson Architects, 2001

A stone, wood, and stucco house in Stinson's signature layered style. The L-shaped house is nicely sited on its narrow lot to take advantage of lake views.

22 V. Mel and Henet Kaufman House *L*

20 Park Ln.

James Brunet, 1936

A significant early work of modernist architecture in the Twin Cities. The house's ribbonlike arrangement of windows (specially made by the Andersen Corp. in Bayport, MN), the smooth stucco walls, and the boxy massing (though there are some curves to the rear) are all drawn from the modernist vocabulary,

V. Mel and Henet Kaufman House

as is the flat roof. Architect James Brunet was among the first graduates of the University of Minnesota's architecture school to have been indoctrinated with modernist ideas, and he was fortunate to find clients who shared his tastes. Salesman V. Mel Kaufman and his wife had visited the 1933 Century of Progress Exposition in Chicago, where futuristic design was on display, and it convinced them to build a thoroughly modern house of their own.

POI C Cedar Lake

Minneapolis Park Board, 1908 and later

Cedar seems at first glance to be the "wildest" of the Minneapolis lakes, but it's actually the product of much manipulation by railways, road builders, and dredgers. Most of the lake's original marshy shoreline and its only island were lost in the process. The first railway line cut along the lake's eastern shore in 1867, and two other lines soon followed, as did a resort hotel in 1870. The Minneapolis Park Board acquired its first property on the lake, at the southern end, in 1908. Three years later the board began dredging the lake to deepen it and create a more stable shoreline. In 1991 the board substantially expanded its holdings with the purchase of 18 acres on the northeast side of the lake formerly occupied by the Minneapolis and St. Louis Railroad shop and yards. Cedar's southeastern side, however, remains unique among the city's lakes in that private lots come right up to the shore, with no intervening parkway. Because streetcar lines never came close enough to provide convenient service, most housing around the lake dates from the automobile age—1920 and later.

POI D Bike trails

Various rail corridors

An outstanding feature of the Lake District is the system of trails that thread through the neighborhood along old rail corridors. The Cedar Lake Trail, established in 1995, follows a former Great Northern (now Burlington Northern Santa Fe) right-of-way. The Kenilworth Trail, which cuts between Cedar Lake and Lake of the Isles, is built along an old route of the Chicago and North Western Railroad. It connects to yet another rail corridor trail—the Midtown Greenway—that follows a former Milwaukee Road line.

23 George and Frances Reid House

3114 28th St. West

Molly Reid (Los Angeles), 2004

A colorful house, clearly under the influence of Frank Gehry and other California modernists. Built for the architect's parents, the house has sculpted volumes, an eclectic mix of cladding materials, eccentric window shapes, and an angular metal roof, all set behind a brick screen formed by portions of an old commercial storefront that once occupied the site.

24 Fleisher Duplexes

2801, 2805 Xerxes Ave. South

Perry Crosier, 1936

Fleisher Duplex

A pair of stuccoed duplexes with corner windows, stepped-down staircases, and projecting balconies. Not as exciting as, say, Miami Beach's tropical deco, but pretty jazzy for Minnesota.

25 3141 Dean Court (grain elevators)

3141 Dean Ct.

McKenzie-Hague Co., 1915–28 / renovated, Brantingham Architects, 1982–85

This is the first—and so far the only—example in the Twin Cities of concrete grain silos being converted into housing. It wasn't done with much panache, however, and instead of celebrating the historic silos, the architects did their best to cover them up.

NowHaus01

26 NowHaus01

3440 St. Paul Ave.

1952 / rebuilt, Locus Architecture (Wynne Yelland and Paul Neseth), 2004

This house, built up from a 1950s rambler, garnered reams of publicity when it appeared in all its high-tech splendor on an otherwise ordinary residential block. It employs novel materials such as siding made from the vinyl used for billboards, and it's also full of trendy design features like a lattice screen that obscures the front door. In view of the house's many unorthodoxies, it's no surprise that it took quite awhile to sell and fetched considerably less than the initial asking price of $1 million. Still, if not for young architects exploring new ideas, the world of design would be very dull indeed.

27 House

3523 Cedar Lake Ave.

1973

The streets around Cedar Lake offer an assortment of what look to be architect-designed modern houses. This one features multiple levels, lots of glass and concrete, and an inset corner tower with finlike projections at the top.

Oak Grove House, 1870

erty in the 1880s to Edward Jones. Later, Jones's mother-in-law, Jane T. Harrison, left a bequest to establish a home for women in the old hotel, which stood until 1892, when it was replaced by a larger building.

Aaron and Naomi Friedell House

28 Aaron and Naomi Friedell House *L*

2700 Chowen Ave. South

Norman R. Johnson, 1940

An interesting Moderne-style house. Aaron Friedell was a physician who helped develop the first health maintenance organization in the Twin Cities. His wife, Naomi, was a sculptor. It appears both worked closely with St. Paul architect Norman Johnson in designing the house.

29 Jones-Harrison Residence

3700 Cedar Lake Ave.

1959 and later

A residential complex for the elderly, founded in 1888 and now occupying one of the oldest building sites on Cedar Lake.

LOST 2 *This was the site of the* **Oak Grove House,** *a resort hotel built in 1870. Located only a few blocks from the tracks of the Minneapolis and St. Louis Railroad, the octagonal three-story hotel offered its patrons a large open porch with vistas of the lake. Its original owners—Reverend Ebenezer Scott and his wife, Gertrude—sold the prop-*

2500 Cedar Shore Dr.

30 House

2500 Cedar Shore Dr.

1961

A sprawling one-story house in the manner of Frank Lloyd Wright. Clad in Mankato-Kasota stone, the house has broad overhanging eaves, long ribbons of windows, and other Wrightian features. At the rear there's a sunken courtyard bordered by a stone wall.

POI E Brownie Lake

Named after the daughter of an early settler, this ten-acre lake was once considerably larger. Portions of it were filled in by railroad and highway construction in the late nineteenth century. The lake shrank to its present size in 1917, when it was connected to Cedar Lake by a channel, causing the water level to drop by nine feet.

31 Target Financial Services (Prudential Building)

3701 Wayzata Blvd.

Magney Tusler and Setter, 1954

An important but often overlooked example of 1950s corporate architecture, built as a regional home office for the Prudential Insurance Co. The building, which goes about its corporate business in a refined

Target Financial Services

if not especially exciting way, is notable for the clarity with which it expresses its functions. The main offices are grouped into three wings, ranging in height from four to eight stories, that splay off a central ten-story core. Clad in Mankato-Kasota stone, these wings have slightly projecting square windows that march across the facades with military precision, conveying an image of corporate rationalism and modernity. The central core and an auditorium wing have few windows, by contrast, and are sheathed in pink granite. The building also benefits from its

pastoral setting on a 30-acre site that was once part of Theodore Wirth Park. The Minneapolis Park Board sold the property to Prudential and used the proceeds to purchase additional shoreland around Cedar Lake. The land sale sparked a legal challenge that was ultimately settled in the board's favor by the Minnesota Supreme Court.

Arvid Bjorklund House

32 Arvid Bjorklund House

1204 Cedar Lake Rd.

1927

A split-level house in a style that might be called Mediterranean Moderne. There's a similar house just a few doors down at 1224 Cedar Lake Rd.

Kenwood, Cedar-Isles

Lake Calhoun and Uptown

This neighborhood is the most varied in the Lake District. Here you'll find the city's largest lake, a broad mix of homes and apartments, an old rail and industrial corridor that's attracted much new condominium development, and, of course, the Uptown district with its conglomeration of shops, restaurants, and theaters.

At the center of it all is Lake Calhoun. While the city's other lakes are ensconced in exclusively residential neighborhoods, Calhoun is bordered on the north by Lake Street, a wide and heavily traveled thoroughfare. Commercial buildings and residential towers, including the historic Vintage Apartments (built as the Calhoun Beach Club in 1928), loom over this end of the lake, which offers a full frontal view of the downtown skyline. The result is that Calhoun has a more jangly, big-city feel than any of the other Minneapolis lakes. It's a bit quieter along the southern and western shores, where the usual complement of expensive homes drink in the scenery.

Just to the east of the lake is the thriving Uptown area, where the look ranges from chic to punk and the action goes on well into the night. What might be called the modern era of Uptown's development began in the early 1980s when the Calhoun Square shopping mall opened at Hennepin and Lake. More recently, scores of new condominiums, apartments, restaurants, and shops have added to Uptown's vitality—and traffic. The Calhoun-Uptown area also had an industrial zone at one time along the old Milwaukee Road tracks— today's Midtown Greenway—paralleling 29th Street. A number of former factories still stand here, including the Buzza Co. Building (1907 and later), now a school.

The residential neighborhoods to the east of Lake Calhoun are generally quite modest. Here, early twentieth-century houses and walk-up apartment buildings predominate. The western side of the lake, near the city limits, has some larger homes, including the Goodfellow House (1930), now a museum. Much of this choice area is taken up by the Minikahda Country Club (1899), the city's oldest golf course.

POI A Lake Calhoun parks and parkway

Minneapolis Park Board, 1886 and later

Named in 1817 after U.S. secretary of war John C. Calhoun (who authorized construction of Fort Snelling), this 422-acre lake was known to the Dakota as *Mde Medoza* (Lake of the Loons). The first year-round settlement, on the eastern shore, was Cloud Man's Village, established in 1828. Brothers Samuel and Gideon Pond built a cabin nearby six years later. Both the village and the cabin were gone by 1840. The lake area remained largely unpopulated until the 1870s, when resort hotels sprang up on the eastern and western shores. Later, at least two companies began harvesting ice from the lake and built unsightly sheds that stood along the northern shore until 1909. For the most part, however, the lake was undeveloped when the Minneapolis Park Board began acquiring land around it in 1886. By 1909, the board had control of the entire lake and 89 acres of shoreland, for a cost of just $127,000.

Although a naturally deep lake, Calhoun's original shoreline was marshy, and today's parkways and beaches were made possible by dredging operations undertaken between 1911 and 1915 and again in the 1920s. All told, the park board's dredging crews removed more than a million cubic yards of material from the lake and redeposited it along the shore. A channel linking Calhoun to Lake of the Isles was completed in 1911.

Lake Calhoun

Vintage Apartments

1 Vintage Apartments (Calhoun Beach Club) N

2925 Dean Pkwy.

Charles W. Nicol (Chicago) with Magney and Tusler, 1928–46 / renovated, 1977 / renovated, ESG Architects, 2002

In the early 1920s, Minneapolis businessman Harry S. Goldie conceived the idea for a swank club and residential building over-looking Lake Calhoun. Goldie and other promoters of the project began soliciting memberships, and by 1928 he'd raised enough capital to begin construction of this building, at the time the tallest in the city outside the downtown core. Chicago architect Charles W. Nicol designed the Calhoun Beach Club in the fashionable Renaissance Revival style. Goldie's timing, however, was less than perfect. The stock market crashed just as the building was nearing completion in 1929, and it stood vacant until after World War II. When it finally opened in 1946, the building consisted of ground-floor commercial space, club facilities (including a swimming pool, gymnasium, and ballroom) on the lower three floors, and apartments and one floor of hotel rooms above. In 2002, the club, now the Vintage Apartments, was extensively renovated; today it includes luxury apartments as well as a health club, retail space, and meeting rooms.

2 Calhoun Beach Club Apartments

2900 Thomas Ave. South

KKE Architects, 1999

This 12-story apartment complex is located just to the east of the Vintage Apartments. It's an ex-ample of what might be called the Beau Brummel Style: an archi-tectural dandy that offers plenty of flash but that's clad in such thin material you have to wonder how long it will be before it begins to look threadbare.

*LOST 1 The north shore of Lake Calhoun was once the site of a large **bathhouse**. Built in 1912, it was a Spanish-Moorish concoction with a twin-towered central pavilion flanked by large changing rooms. These were open to the sky, thereby affording residents who moved into the upper floors of the Calhoun Beach Club an interesting view. It didn't last for long: four years after the club opened in 1946, the bath-house was demolished, and no trace of it remains today.*

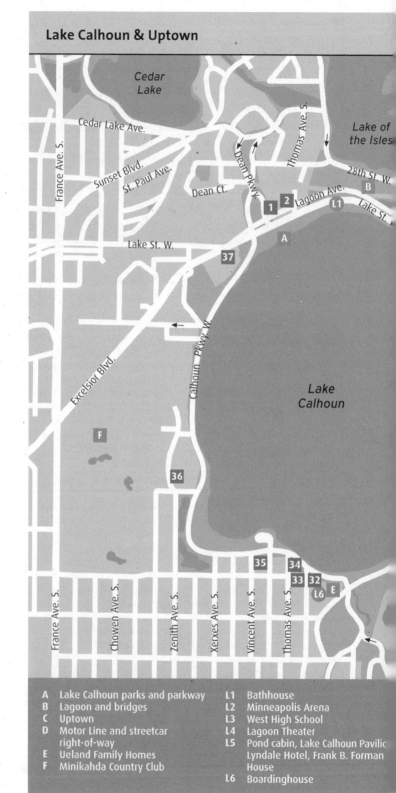

Lake Calhoun & Uptown

Cedar Lake

Cedar Lake Ave.

France Ave. S.

Sunset Blvd.

St. Paul Ave.

Dean Ct.

Dean Pkwy.

Thomas Ave. S.

Lake of the Isles

28th St. W.

B

Lagoon Ave.

1 **2**

L1

Lake St.

A

Lake St. W.

37

Calhoun Pkwy. W.

Excelsior Blvd.

F

Lake Calhoun

36

35 **34**

33 **32**

L6 **E**

France Ave. S.

Chowen Ave. S.

Zenith Ave. S.

Xerxes Ave. S.

Vincent Ave. S.

Thomas Ave. S.

A	Lake Calhoun parks and parkway	**L1**	Bathhouse
B	Lagoon and bridges	**L2**	Minneapolis Arena
C	Uptown	**L3**	West High School
D	Motor Line and streetcar right-of-way	**L4**	Lagoon Theater
E	Ueland Family Homes	**L5**	Pond cabin, Lake Calhoun Pavilic Lyndale Hotel, Frank B. Forman House
F	Minikahda Country Club		
		L6	Boardinghouse

Vintage Apartments	**20** Apartments
Calhoun Beach Club Apartments	**21** Joyce Memorial Methodist Church
Edgewater Condominiums	**22** Houses
Condominiums	**23** Calhoun Park Terrace
Moorish Mansion Apartments	**24** Castle Jeweler
Citadel Building	**25** First Universalist Church
Stella's Fish Cafe	**26** Apartment building
Lehmann Education Center	**27** House
Bryant-Lake Bowl	**28** Hennepin Aristocrat Apartments
Crowell Block	**29** House
Track 29 Townhomes and Lofts	**30** House
Granada Apartments	**31** St. Mary's Greek Orthodox Church
J. W. Baxter Building	**32** James Pohlad House
Uptown Transit Station	**33** House
Walker Community Library	**34** House
Old Walker Branch Library	**35** Houses
Uptown Theatre	**36** The Bakken Library and Museum
Calhoun Square	**37** Lake Calhoun Executive Center
Suburban World Theatre	

Bridge over lagoon at Lake St.

POI B Lagoon and bridges

Lagoon between Lake Calhoun and Lake of the Isles

Minneapolis Park Board, 1911

Bridges at Lake St. and Lake of the Isles Pkwy.

Cowles and Chapman, 1911

The isthmus between Lake Calhoun and Lake of the Isles was once a swampy lowland. Partially filled in by the construction of railroad tracks in the 1880s, it assumed its present configuration in 1911, when the Minneapolis Park Board completed the channel and small lagoon that now connect the two lakes. This work was part of a project that also entailed dredging and reshaping Lake of the Isles. To span the new channel here, as well as another that would soon link Isles to Cedar Lake, new bridges were required. The park board held a design competition for these structures. William Cowles and Cecil B. Chapman of Minneapolis won, and their classically inspired concrete-arch bridges are still in service today. The bridge at Lake St. features an elliptical arch faced in two types of granite. Other bridges are clad in limestone and include balustrades and ornamental keystones.

3 Edgewater Condominiums

1805 Lake St. West

ESG Architects, 2006

A chunky six-story condominium building that would have looked better had it been taller and thinner. But residents in most Twin Cities neighborhoods have become averse to height, making slender residential towers all but impossible to build outside of downtown areas.

4 Condominiums

3033 Calhoun Pkwy. East

Richard F. Zenisek, 1973

An angular building sheathed in wood. The sawtooth profile assures that each apartment has a good view of the lake.

Moorish Mansion Apartments

5 Moorish Mansion Apartments *L*

3028 James Ave. South

Carl J. Bard, 1929

Apartment buildings from the 1920s offer a salmagundi of styles, the more exotic the better. Here the look is Islamic Revival, done with considerable flair.

6 Citadel Building (Salvation Army Hall)

1516 Lake St. West

Clyde W. Smith, 1925

A two-story Renaissance Revival building with a shallow central pediment and cast-stone and tile trim. It was built for the Salvation Army, whose logo can be seen in a medallion near the peak of the pediment.

POI C Uptown

Area centering around Lake St. West and Hennepin Ave.

Although there's no official Minneapolis neighborhood called "Uptown," the area around Lake St. and Hennepin Ave. has been known by this name since at least the 1920s. Once a major streetcar transfer point, the intersection is now at the center of what might be called Minneapolis's *other* downtown—

home to shops, clubs, restaurants, and theaters, along with a growing number of apartments and condominiums. Uptown wasn't always such a bustling place, however, largely because of a city decision in 1884 to restrict commercial development along Hennepin by designating it a parkway south of downtown. As more people poured into the Lake District, commercial pressures grew, and in 1905 the city finally pulled the cork from the bottle, ending Hennepin's days as a parkway. Entrepreneurs rushed in to fill the void, and by the 1920s several hundred businesses were operating in the vicinity of Hennepin and Lake. Like other urban areas, Uptown declined in the 1950s and 1960s. The opening of Calhoun Square shopping mall in 1983 helped revitalize the neighborhood, which is now among the busiest places in the Twin Cities.

7 Stella's Fish Cafe (Calhoun Theater)

1402 Lake St. West

Clifford McElroy, 1915 and later

Behind all the stucco here lie the remains of the Calhoun Theater, which had a patterned brick facade and elegant Italian Romanesque detailing. The building went through a number of uses before taking on its present incarnation as a seafood restaurant.

Lehmann Education Center

8 Lehmann Education Center (Buzza Co. Building)

1006 Lake St. West

1907 / additions, Magney and Tusler, 1923–27 / renovated, 1971 and later

This concrete and brick industrial building, mildly Classical Revival in style, is among the largest structures in Uptown. The oldest portion dates to 1907 and was originally built for the Self-Threading Needle Co. It was purchased in 1923 by the Buzza Co., once the nation's second-largest maker of greeting cards and calendars. The company's namesake and founder, George Buzza, was a commercial artist who produced posters before branching out into the greeting card business in 1909. Buzza brought in talented artists to design his company's cards, which were known for their rich colors. He also hired popular poets, Edgar Guest among them, to endow the cards with memorable sentiments.

The company grew rapidly and enlarged this building three times in the 1920s. Most of it was loft space, but the upper floors once included elegant offices and showrooms furnished with Italian antiques. The company merged with a New York firm in 1928 to become the Buzza-Clark Co., and Buzza himself retired to California the next year. The company's fortunes sank during the Great Depression, and it went out of business in 1942, when the federal government acquired the building. The government sold it in 1971 to the Minneapolis Public Schools, which two years later turned it into an education center.

9 Bryant-Lake Bowl

810 Lake St. West

ca. 1900 and later

This establishment, which includes a cabaret-style theater and restaurant in addition to eight lanes for the kegling crowd, is one of the Twin Cities' oldest bowling alleys. Its retro quality makes it very popular with the younger set.

10 Crowell Block *L*

614 Lake St. West

Joralemon and Ferrin, 1888 / renovated, Dovolis Johnson and Ruggieri, 1990

A Richardsonian Romanesque building that features rusticated sandstone facades, bay and arched windows, and a heavy stone parapet. With its broad windows and narrow piers, the

Crowell Block

building has a more open, cellular look than is typical of the Richardsonian style. Frank Crowell, after whom the building is named, was a real estate developer.

11 Track 29 Townhomes and Lofts

Aldrich and Bryant Aves. South north of 29th St. West

Aaron Parker (townhomes) and Nelson Tremain Partnership (lofts), 2006

Midtown Lofts

Bryant and Colfax Aves. South north of 29th St. West

ESG Architects, 2004

These stucco-, brick-, and metal-clad apartments and townhomes eschew nostalgia and should be hip enough to attract the Uptown crowd.

LOST 2 *Where Uptown Rainbow Foods stands at 1104 Lagoon Ave. was from 1920 to 1965 the site of the* **Minneapolis Arena.** *Never much to look at, the 5,000-seat arena was used primarily for hockey and ice events but also did occasional duty as a ballroom. The Ice Follies, founded by three Minneapolis men, got its start at the arena in the 1930s.*

12 Granada Apartments

1456 Lagoon Ave.

Carl J. Bard, 1929

It's said that the Islamic look of many buildings in the 1920s was

Granada Apartments

influenced by the popularity of silent film star Rudolph Valentino, who did several turns as a sheik during his brief career. Be that as it may, this apartment building does a nice Spanish-Moorish turn of its own. The building's loveliest feature is an arcaded front courtyard.

13 J. W. Baxter Building

2748–56 Hennepin Ave.

Jenson and Foss, 1927

A charming little commercial building dominated by arched windows with circling bricks laid in such a way that they almost look wedged into place. There's also plenty of stone and terracotta trim, not to mention spiral pinnacles along the roofline.

West High School, 1910

LOST 3 *The Kenwood Isles Condominiums, built in 1986 at 1425 28th St. West, occupy the site of* **West High School.** *The brick and stone school, built to accommodate more than 1,000 students, was a sturdy Classical Revival design featuring large arched entries to either side of a pedimented central pavilion. As with other schools of its period, West conveyed a sense of stateliness and permanence. But the latter proved elusive, as it always does. The school closed its doors in 1982 and was demolished two years later.*

14 Uptown Transit Station

Hennepin Ave. at 29th St. over
Midtown Greenway

LSA Design, 2001

A zippy brick, glass, and steel transit station with a cable-supported
roof and a clock tower that will
let you know you've just missed
your bus.

15 Walker Community Library

2880 Hennepin Ave.

*Myers and Bennett and BRW
Architects, 1981 / renovated,
Bonestroo, Rosene, Anderlik
and Associates, 2004*

The energy crunch of the 1970s
prompted much interest in underground buildings. Here's an example: a library for bookworms
who like to burrow. The two
main floors are set below grade
and overlook a sunken courtyard.
An entry pavilion with a large
"library" sign pops up on Hennepin to let you know there's a
building somewhere below.

16 Old Walker Branch Library *L*

2901 Hennepin Ave.

*Jerome Paul Jackson, 1911 /
remodeled, 1984*

A Classical Revival building constructed of light brown Roman
brick with limestone trim. It was
last used as a library in 1980, just
before its replacement opened
across the street. As of 2008, the
building was vacant and waiting to
be adopted by a loving new owner.

17 Uptown Theatre *i*

2906 Hennepin Ave.

*Liebenberg and Kaplan, 1939 /
remodeled, 1968 / Art: murals,
Gustave Krollman, 1939*

The city's last single-screen movie
house, and a fine example of the
Moderne style from the prolific
drafting board of Jack Liebenberg, the Twin Cities' greatest
theater architect. The Uptown,
which has survived by showing
art films and the like, features

upper walls of Mankato-Kasota
stone punctuated by an exclamation point in the form of a 50-
foot-high vertical sign. Originally
fitted out with a searchlight, the

Uptown Theatre

sign is a dramatic presence along
Hennepin. Also accenting the
theater's otherwise plain facades
are two exquisite bas-relief sculptures framed within circles. Inside,
the lobby has been compromised
by a 1960s remodeling, but the
900-seat auditorium retains two
wonderfully corny murals by
Gustave Krollman, the best of
which depicts bare-breasted
maidens pouring water from one
city lake into another until it all
empties into the Mississippi.
Compare this artistic delight to
what passes for decoration in
movie houses today, and you'll
understand why people love old
theaters.

LOST 4 *The first movie house here
was the **Lagoon Theater,** a Classical
Revival–style building that opened
in 1913 and included a second-floor
dance hall. The theater was remodeled and renamed the Uptown in
1929 but was demolished ten years
later after a fire.*

18 Calhoun Square

3001 Hennepin Ave. (at Lake St.)

*Paul Pink and Associates, 1983 /
incorporates older buildings,
including the **Geanakoplos Building,** Adam Lansing Dorr, 1917*

A classic project from the early
1980s, a time when significant
tax credits became available and
there was renewed public interest in historic preservation. As a
design, this atrium-style indoor

mall, built from a group of old buildings, isn't especially impressive—except perhaps for its splendid rooftop sign. Even so, the mall played a critical role in

Calhoun Square

launching a new wave of development in Uptown. Given how many malls of this kind have failed, the fact that Calhoun Square is still around also ranks as an accomplishment. Work on various improvements to the mall, including added parking, began in 2008.

19 Suburban World (Granada) Theatre i

3022 Hennepin Ave.

Liebenberg and Kaplan, 1928 / remodeled, 1954, 1966

One of Uptown's great delights, this movie house, built as the Granada, is the last operating example in the Twin Cities of a so-called "atmospheric" theater. Although the original lobby and entrances were remodeled out of existence in 1966, much of Liebenberg and Kaplan's design remains intact, including the upper portions of the front facade,

Suburban World Theatre

decorated in an exotic style known as Spanish Churrigueresque Revival.

The real fun, however, lies within. Here you'll find an "atmospheric" auditorium, the invention of a St. Louis architect named John Eberson. His idea, first applied to a theater in Houston in 1923, was designed to convey a sense of being outside at night in a romantic, Old World setting. Eberson wrote, "We visualize and dream a magnificent amphitheater, an Italian garden, a Persian court, a Spanish patio, or a mystic Egyptian templeyard, all canopied by a soft moonlight sky." In the case of the Granada, Liebenberg and Kaplan opted for the Spanish patio. Balconies, balustrades, and arched doorways rise like stage sets along both sides of the auditorium. Above, twinkling stars and drifting clouds are projected across the ceiling. It's indeed "atmospheric," and still a wonderful way to spend a night at the movies.

Suburban World Theatre interior

20 Apartments

3100 Girard Ave. South

1969

This apartment building adds a Moorish Revival twist to its otherwise bland 1960s modernism. The result can best be described as mighty peculiar.

21 Joyce Memorial Methodist Church

1219 31st St. West

Downs and Eads, 1907

Established in 1886 as a mission, this church was renamed in 1905 after a Methodist bishop, Isaac Joyce, who died while delivering a fire-and-brimstone sermon at a revival meeting. This stucco church is one of the more thoroughgoing local examples of the California Mission look, complete with a three-stage tower, sculpted parapets, and tile roofs. The sun-kissed Mission Style isn't one you'd normally associate with the rigorous tenets of Methodism, but the Joyce congregation obviously warmed to it.

22 Houses

3136, 3140, 3142 Colfax Ave. South

ca. 1883–85

Three working-class homes that must have been all but identical originally. The L shape and narrow front profile are characteristic of vernacular housing in the 1880s.

23 Calhoun Park Terrace

3013–23 Aldrich Ave. South

1888

One of the few row houses in the Lake District. The style seems to be a blend of Queen Anne and Romanesque Revival. Another row house stands a few blocks away, at 3310–20 Humboldt Ave. South.

24 Castle Jeweler (White Castle Building No. 8) N *L*

3252 Lyndale Ave. South

L. W. Ray, 1936

The oldest home of little square hamburgers in the Twin Cities, now selling gems instead of gut bombs. The White Castle chain, founded in Kansas in 1921, had by the 1930s become such a large operation that it maintained its own fabricating plant, where this 840-square-foot porcelain-steel

Castle Jeweler

building was made. It's one of only a half dozen or so White Castle buildings of this type left in the United States. After being shipped to Minneapolis, the building was erected in 1936 at 616 Washington Ave. Southeast. It stood there until 1950, when it was dismantled and reassembled at 329 Central Ave. Southeast. White Castle closed the restaurant in 1983. Preservationists working with the city saved the structure from demolition and moved it here.

25 First Universalist Church (Adath Jeshurun Synagogue) *L*

3400 Dupont Ave. South

Liebenberg and Kaplan, 1927 / additions, Liebenberg and Kaplan, 1954 and later

This stately Renaissance Revival–style building was constructed for Adath Jeshurun, founded in 1884 by immigrants from Eastern Europe and said to be the oldest Conservative Jewish congregation west of Chicago. As built, the synagogue could seat 1,200 for services and included a theater and classrooms. Adath Jeshurun moved to a new synagogue in suburban Minnetonka in the early 1990s and sold this building to the First Universalist Church.

26 Apartment building

3452 Emerson Ave. South

1969

Mansard roofs of ridiculous size sprouted like bad hairdos on

3452 Emerson Ave. South

many apartment buildings constructed in the 1960s and 1970s. Here's a classic of the kind, done in a screaming blue so you can't miss it.

27 House

3554 Girard Ave. South

1950

A modernist house with vertical wood siding and the inevitable flat roof. There's an interesting panel with carved floral motifs next to the house's entry off Girard.

Hennepin Aristocrat Apartments

28 Hennepin Aristocrat Apartments

3332 Hennepin Ave.

Liebenberg and Kaplan, 1961

The architectural equivalent of a loud sport coat—the kind, say, a car salesman might have worn in the old days of tail fins and V-8s. High-toned 1960s modernists of the less-is-more school must have been appalled by the building's multicolored brick facade, which also offers gaudy grill-like panels made from patterned concrete blocks. But if you are sensible enough to enjoy the sweet aroma of kitsch when it wafts your way, then you will adore this building, designed by theater architects who knew how to put on a good show.

POI D Motor Line and streetcar right-of-way

Alley in block bounded by 32nd and 34th Sts., Irving Ave. South, and Calhoun Pkwy. East

1879 and later

Go down this long alley and you'll discover that most of the garages on the west side are set back much farther than you'd expect them to be. The reason for this anomaly is that the alley occupies part of what was once a 33-foot-wide private right-of-way, used first by the Minneapolis, Lyndale and Lake Calhoun Railway (the Motor Line) and later by Twin City Rapid Transit Co. streetcars. When the streetcar era came to an end in the early 1950s, the tracks were removed and the right-of-way vacated.

29 House

3247 Calhoun Pkwy. East

ca. 1900

Most of the older houses on Lake Calhoun are along the eastern shore. This one has a side tower and concrete block walls with a sandstone-like veneer laid up in an interlocking pattern.

30 House

3424 Humboldt Ave. South

1946

A two-story Moderne box with rose-colored concrete trim. It includes one odd feature: a small side gable that projects from what otherwise appears to be a flat roof.

St. Mary's Greek Orthodox Church

31 St. Mary's Greek Orthodox Church

3450 Irving Ave. South

Thorshov and Cerny, 1957 / addition, Chris Kamagais, 2001

Occupying a historic site overlooking Lake Calhoun, this

church blends traditional and modern elements. The Greek cross shape and a golden dome are common features of Orthodox churches, but here they're combined with crisply detailed brickwork and a glass-walled entry typical of 1950s modernism. An events center that includes a great hall, meeting rooms, and a courtyard was added in 2001.

Lyndale Hotel, 1880

LOST 5 *St. Mary's stands on a site with a long history of buildings. In the courtyard, a bronze plaque set in a boulder commemorates the **Pond cabin,** built by brothers Samuel and Gideon in 1834. The next occupant of note in the area was William King, whose 1,400-acre Lyndale Farm included this site. In 1879, coinciding with completion of the Motor Line from downtown, King built his **Lake Calhoun Pavilion** at this location. The multistory, all-wood structure offered verandas facing the lake. By the early 1880s, after various real estate perturbations, developer Louis Menage took over the pavilion and renamed it the **Lyndale Hotel.** In an era of cigar smoking, oil lamps, and open flames, wooden hotels were notoriously prone to combustion, and the Lyndale burned down in 1888. The site then remained vacant until 1901, when the **Frank B. Forman House** appeared. Forman, who founded a paint and glass company, built the 20-room mansion for himself and his wife. The Classical Revival–style home featured a two-story-high entrance porch and views of the lake. Forman died in 1912, but his wife, an eccentric woman known for her kindness to neighborhood children, lived in the house until her death in 1949. The house was demolished six years later. An insurance company*

made plans for an office structure on the site, but neighbors were opposed, and in the end St. Mary's acquired the property for its church.

POI E Ueland Family Homes

Calhoun Pkwy. West and Richfield Rd.

1890 and later

In 1890 Andreas and Clara Ueland built a 16-room Colonial Revival house on a site wedged between Calhoun Pkwy. and Richfield Rd. He was a Norwegian immigrant who'd risen from being a ditchdigger to a position as a probate court judge. She was a teacher who later served as the first president of the Minnesota League of Women Voters. Their eight children included three Nordicly named sons—Sigurd, Rolf, and Arnulf—who in the 1920s built the houses at 3832, 3846, and 3850 Richfield Rd. But it was one of the couple's daughters, Brenda Ueland, who became best known. A talented writer and certified free spirit, she moved to New York City in the 1920s and produced articles for the *Saturday Evening Post, Ladies' Home Journal,* and other magazines. After returning home in 1930, she wrote for the *Minneapolis Times* and later published two books, including a 1939 autobiography entitled *Me.* The Andreas and Clara Ueland House was torn down in 1953. The condominiums and townhomes at 3810 and 3830–32 Calhoun Pkwy. West now occupy the site. Brenda Ueland continued to live nearby until her death, at age 93, in 1985.

LOST 6 *Before Andreas and Clara Ueland built their home here, the property was the site of a **boardinghouse** operated by a certain Mrs. Elizabeth Hamilton. It's not clear when the establishment was built, but it is known that Henry David Thoreau, author of* Walden, *stayed at Mrs. Hamilton's during his visit to the Lake District in June 1861.*

James Pohlad House

32 James Pohlad House

3802 Calhoun Pkwy. West
(also 3811 Sheridan Ave. South)

Charles R. Stinson Architects, 2008

A large, layered house faced in Mankato-Kasota stone. Many of the recent infill homes in the Lake District have been of the McMansion variety, but here a sense of sleek modernism prevails.

3790 Calhoun Pkwy. West

33 House

3790 Calhoun Pkwy. West

Benjamin Gingold, 1957

An interesting 1950s house that calls to mind the domestic work of Marcel Breuer, best known in Minnesota as the architect of the Abbey Church (1961) at St. John's University. The house's lower floor is clad in gray fieldstone and has a quiet demeanor. The stuccoed second floor, on the other hand, juts out aggressively and offers a view of the lake through a long wraparound window set within a heavy frame.

34 House

3766 Calhoun Pkwy. West

ca. 1860s and later

Portions of this house, which shows traces of the Greek Revival style, may date to the 1860s,

when the property was acquired by a carpenter named Ezra Hamilton. If so, it's the oldest house on Lake Calhoun. But the evidence is sketchy, and it's possible this house wasn't built until the 1880s or later.

35 Houses

3742, 3744, 3746 Calhoun Pkwy. West

2000–2001

Any time a lot becomes available in the Lake District these days, it's quickly filled by a big new house. These three homes are among the latest additions to the lakeside scene. The houses at 3744 and 3746 wisely adhere to a modernist aesthetic, but 3742 goes in for some sort of Italian palazzo look, with predictably unhappy results.

The Bakken Library and Museum

36 The Bakken Library and Museum (William Goodfellow House, "West Winds")

3537 Zenith Ave. South

Carl Gage, 1930 / addition, MS&R Architects, 1998

Focusing on the role of electricity and magnetism in medicine, this museum occupies what was once Lake Calhoun's grandest house, built—so it's said—for love. Local lore holds that William Goodfellow (whose family money came in part from the sale of a dry goods store to George Dayton) constructed the 15-room mansion, which he called "West Winds," to impress a woman he hoped to marry. With that romantic object in mind, Goodfellow did not stint on the details. Surrounded by an eight-foot-high wall, the house and its grounds, including a garden designed by landscape architect Michael Swingley, have the feel of a country estate. The mansion's stone, stucco, and half-timbered exterior is fairly conventional Tudor Revival, although well and expensively done. Inside, however, Goodfellow and architect Carl Gage pulled out all the stops. There's a Tudor-style great hall, much dark paneling, and fine woodcarving executed by craftsmen. Nor did Goodfellow have far to go to reach a bathroom: the house had 11, a rooms-to-toilets ratio perhaps unequaled by any other mansion in the Twin Cities. Alas, Goodfellow's building campaign didn't win over the woman of his dreams, and he died in 1944, presumably unrequited.

The house had two subsequent owners before it was sold in 1976 to the Bakken. The museum and library were established by Earl Bakken, cofounder of Medtronic Corp., a Twin Cities–based company known for its cardiac pacemakers. In 1998 the Minneapolis firm of Meyer, Scherer and Rockcastle designed a 12,000-foot addition that nearly doubled the size of the museum and that blends seamlessly with the original house.

POI F Minikahda Country Club

Includes **clubhouse,** 3205 Excelsior Blvd.

Long and Long, 1899, 1902 / numerous additions / renovated, Partners and Sirny, 1995

Established in 1898 on a low bluff overlooking Lake Calhoun, this is the city's oldest golf course. Its grounds once extended down to the lake, but in 1909 the club donated that part of its land to the Minneapolis Park Board in exchange for the right to pump water from Calhoun, a practice that continued until the 1950s. Minikahda's Classical Revival–style clubhouse dates to 1899 but has several additions. The U.S. Open golf tournament was held here in 1916—the only "major" ever played in Minneapolis.

37 Lake Calhoun Executive Center (American Hardware Mutual Building)

3033 Excelsior Blvd.

1955 / remodeled, 1988

A 1950s office building that received a complete face-lift in the 1980s and now looks as though it would be perfectly at home in a suburban office park.

5 Lake Harriet, East Harriet, and Lynnhurst

Lake Harriet, East Harriet, and Lynnhurst

This part of the Lake District, which includes Lake Harriet and the neighborhoods to the east and south, is almost exclusively residential, and it clearly demonstrates how wealth is drawn to water like a dowsing rod. Near the lake and along Minnehaha Creek you'll encounter block after block of elegant houses ranging from 1880s Victorians to the latest modernist designs. Move a bit farther away from the water, however, and the housing tends to be more modest.

The land around Lake Harriet was acquired by the Minneapolis Park Board in the 1880s. By 1886 the board had built a dirt road around Harriet, making it the first city lake to be ringed by a parkway. Despite this improvement, residential development was retarded by the lake's relative distance from early streetcar lines. This was especially true of the eastern and southern shores, and it wasn't until automobiles arrived in the early twentieth century that houses started to appear all around Harriet.

Most of the big houses that circle the lake date from about 1910 to 1935—the great age of Period Revival architecture. Tudor, Norman, Colonial, and Classical are among the revived styles on display. Most of these houses were designed by local architects, and while there are no masterpieces among them, they display the fine craftsmanship and lively pictorial imagination typical of Period Revival design. You'll also find a smattering of Arts and Crafts houses around the lake.

The housing stock in the East Harriet and Lynnhurst neighborhoods also dates largely from the first two decades of the twentieth century. Among the highlights are five Prairie Style houses designed by William Purcell and George Elmslie between 1910 and 1917. The Charles and Grace Parker House (1913) on Colfax is especially outstanding. Numerous Arts and Crafts and Period Revival–style houses can be found here as well. In addition to its many fine homes, East Harriet is the domain of Lakewood Cemetery, the Twin Cities' preeminent burial ground, established in 1871. Harry Jones's magnificent Memorial Chapel (1910) is Lakewood's chief architectural treasure, but there are also many interesting monuments and mausoleums scattered throughout the cemetery's ample grounds.

POI A Lake Harriet parks and parkways

Minneapolis Park Board, 1880s and later

At 344 acres, Harriet is the second largest of the city's lakes. Insulated by Lyndale Park and Lakewood Cemetery on its north side, Harriet has wooded, steeply banked shores that give it a more "natural" feel than nearby Lake Calhoun. Named after the wife of Colonel Henry Leavenworth, first commandant of Fort Snelling, the lake was known to the Dakota people as *Mde Unma*, or simply "the other lake," a reference to its relationship to Lake Calhoun. Like most Minneapolis lakes, it occupies an old channel of the Mississippi River.

The lake remained largely undeveloped until the 1880s. Among those attracted to its wild beauty was Henry David Thoreau, who visited the area in 1861, a year before his death. In 1880 the Minneapolis, Lyndale and Lake Calhoun Railway (known as the Motor Line) reached the lake's west shore. The railway built a pavilion to attract visitors but never made a profit and abandoned its line in 1886. Five years later, the Twin City Rapid Transit Co. began streetcar service to the lake along the old Motor Line route. By this time, the Minneapolis Park Board had acquired the lake and begun improvements. Harriet was not as heavily dredged as some of the other city lakes, however, and much of the

Lake Harriet

work was along the northern shore, where a marsh was turned into Lyndale Park. After constructing Lake Harriet Pkwy., the board built a picnic pavilion and bandstand on the west shore. Today, the lake continues to be one of the city's most popular attractions.

Lake Harriet Band Shell

1 Women's and Men's Restrooms *L*

Near Lake Harriet Pkwy. West and 42nd St.

Harry Jones, 1891

These small Shingle Style restrooms are the oldest public buildings at Lake Harriet. Their style influenced the design of the nearby band shell and refectory.

2 Lake Harriet Band Shell and Refectory !

4135 Lake Harriet Pkwy. West

Bentz/Thompson/Rietow Architects, 1986 / renovated, 2004

Postmodernism in its dumbed-down, populist phase produced so much dreadful architecture—think of all those 1980s shopping malls outfitted with fake gables—that you can easily forget what the movement was supposed to be about. These wonderful buildings will remind you that at its best postmodernism was an effort to reinfuse architecture with a sense of beauty, memory, and

continuity—qualities that many modernists rejected or simply paid no attention to. Both buildings, which play on the site's rich architectural history (there were three earlier pavilions here), will also remind you that architecture can be flat-out fun. Since its completion in 1986, the band shell has become a civic icon, and rightly so. Clad in shingles, it features a flared arch rising above a steel truss, with steep-roofed towers to either side. Although it's a sophisticated design, the band shell feels as natural as a child's drawing, and it captures the essence of summery delight. The adjacent refectory—a fairy-tale castle in miniature outfitted with six delicate towers that shoot skyward as festively as Fourth of July fireworks—is just as good.

LOST 1 *Three earlier park pavilions occupied this site; all came to disastrous ends. In 1888 the Minneapolis Street Railway Co. erected the* **first pavilion** *along its tracks near Queen Ave. South and*

Lake Harriet, East Harriet, & Lynnhurst

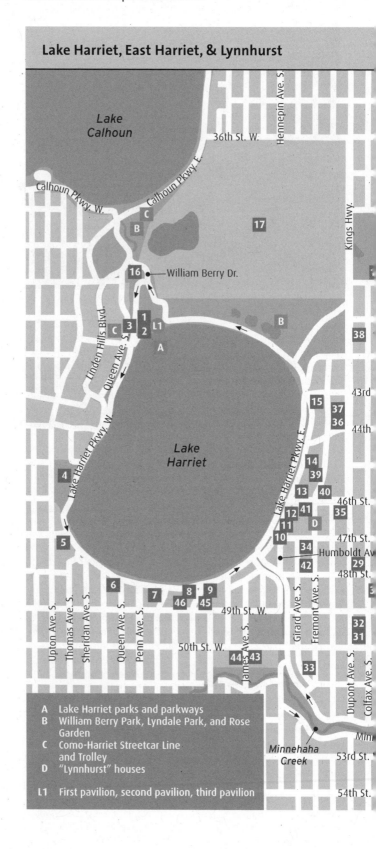

A   Lake Harriet parks and parkways
B   William Berry Park, Lyndale Park, and Rose Garden
C   Como-Harriet Streetcar Line and Trolley
D   "Lynnhurst" houses

L1   First pavilion, second pavilion, third pavilion

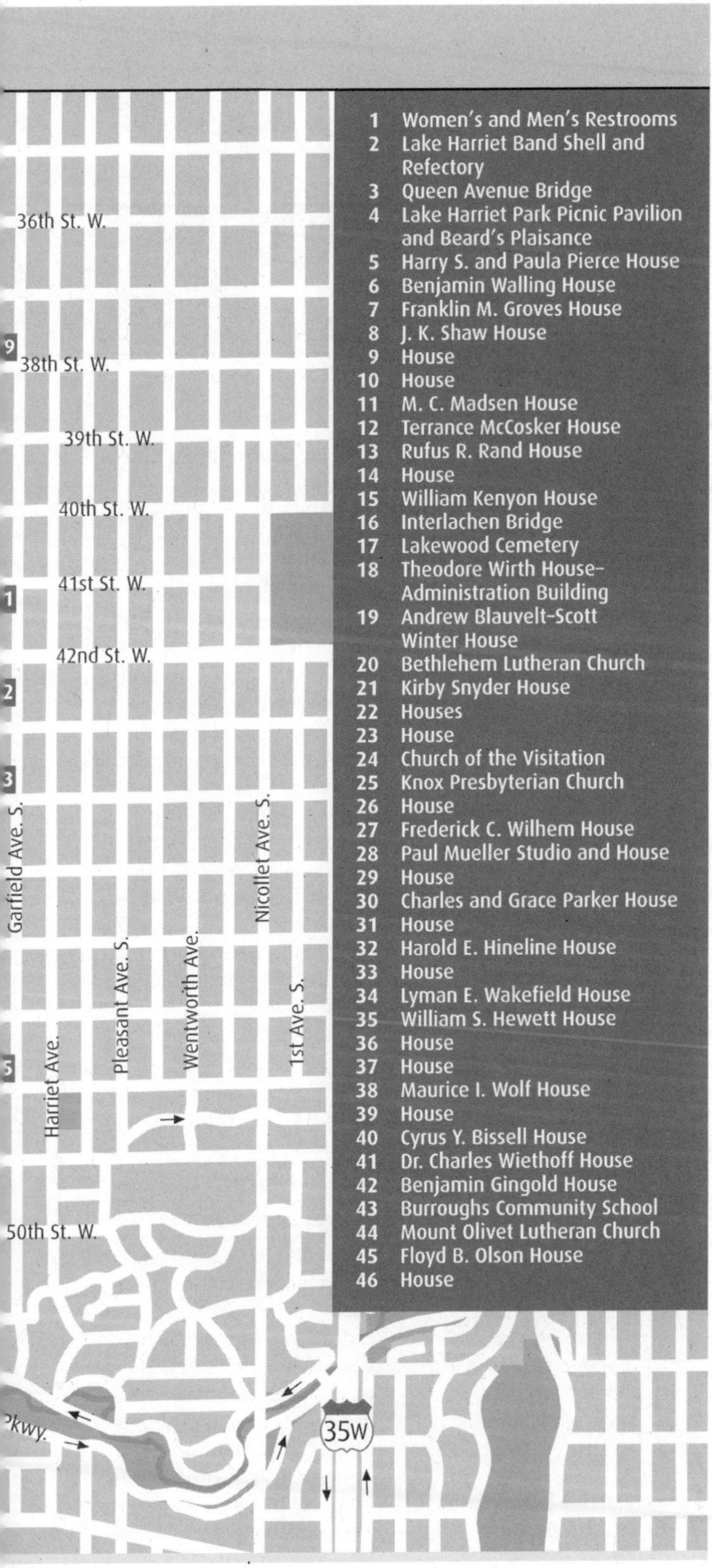

36th St. W.

38th St. W.

39th St. W.

40th St. W.

41st St. W.

42nd St. W.

50th St. W.

Garfield Ave. S.

Harriet Ave.

Pleasant Ave. S.

Wentworth Ave.

Nicollet Ave. S.

1st Ave. S.

Pkwy.

35W

1	Women's and Men's Restrooms
2	Lake Harriet Band Shell and Refectory
3	Queen Avenue Bridge
4	Lake Harriet Park Picnic Pavilion and Beard's Plaisance
5	Harry S. and Paula Pierce House
6	Benjamin Walling House
7	Franklin M. Groves House
8	J. K. Shaw House
9	House
10	House
11	M. C. Madsen House
12	Terrance McCosker House
13	Rufus R. Rand House
14	House
15	William Kenyon House
16	Interlachen Bridge
17	Lakewood Cemetery
18	Theodore Wirth House– Administration Building
19	Andrew Blauvelt–Scott Winter House
20	Bethlehem Lutheran Church
21	Kirby Snyder House
22	Houses
23	House
24	Church of the Visitation
25	Knox Presbyterian Church
26	House
27	Frederick C. Wilhem House
28	Paul Mueller Studio and House
29	House
30	Charles and Grace Parker House
31	House
32	Harold E. Hineline House
33	House
34	Lyman E. Wakefield House
35	William S. Hewett House
36	House
37	House
38	Maurice I. Wolf House
39	House
40	Cyrus Y. Bissell House
41	Dr. Charles Wiethoff House
42	Benjamin Gingold House
43	Burroughs Community School
44	Mount Olivet Lutheran Church
45	Floyd B. Olson House
46	House

Lake Harriet, East Harriet

*42nd St. West. Designed by the Minneapolis firm of Long and Kees, this pavilion was an open, two-story wooden structure that burned down in July 1891. The **second pavilion**, designed by Harry Jones, was a pagodalike wooden structure located directly on the lakeshore, about where the refectory now stands. It survived 12 years before it, too, burned to ashes.*

Lake Harriet Pavilion, 1904

*Jones designed a **third pavilion** on the same spot in 1904. Classical Revival in style, it had two wings that extended out over the lake to shelter a swimming area. There was also a rooftop garden crowned by a circular belvedere that served, none too effectively, as a bandstand. This pavilion stood for just over 20 years before its roof collapsed during a windstorm in July 1925. A hundred or more people were huddled inside when the roof came down, and two of them—a woman and her three-year-old daughter—were killed. After this disaster, the park board decided it had had enough of pavilions and built a small bandstand on the site that was used until the present band shell opened in 1986.*

3 Queen Avenue Bridge N

Lake Harriet Blvd. West at Queen Ave. South over streetcar tracks

Charles Shepley (engineer), 1905

An early reinforced concrete bridge now listed on the National Register of Historic Places.

4 Lake Harriet Park Picnic Pavilion L and Beard's Plaisance

4525 Upton Ave. South

Harry Jones, 1904

This pagodalike picnic pavilion is nestled in a grove of trees at Beard's Plaisance, named after Henry Beard, a real estate developer who donated land for a park here in 1888.

Harry S. and Paula Pierce House, frieze detail

5 Harry S. and Paula Pierce House

4700 Lake Harriet Pkwy. West

Bertrand and Chamberlin, 1910

A taste of Vienna on Lake Harriet. This distinctive house mixes Prairie Style elements, such as the grouped corner windows on the second floor, with Art Nouveau features that appear to be drawn from the contemporaneous Viennese Secession movement in Austria. Secessionist details include segmental arch windows and small outbreaks of tile arranged in geometric patterns that pepper the house's otherwise smooth white walls. The most unusual feature of all is a second-story frieze depicting knights and maidens in a forest scene.

6 Benjamin Walling House L

4850 Lake Harriet Pkwy. West

Magney and Tusler, 1930

An exquisitely detailed brick house that melds Tudor Revival with the English Arts and Crafts style of the 1890s. Architect Gottlieb Magney is best known as a partner in the firm that designed the Foshay Tower, but he was also responsible for a number of fine Period Revival homes in the 1920s and 1930s. The original owner, Benjamin Walling, was in the real estate business and once served as president of the Minneapolis Real Estate Board.

7 Franklin M. Groves House *L*

4885 Lake Harriet Pkwy. East

Carleton W. Farnham, 1928 / addition, 1936

Perhaps the most secretive house on the lake (heavy foliage obscures it in the summer months), this Mediterranean mansion would be perfectly at home in Beverly Hills or Palm Beach. Set on a steep, lushly landscaped lot, the house has the feel of a romantic hideaway, rising in a series of stucco-clad, tile-roofed volumes that culminate in a cupola, which actually serves as the top of an elevator shaft. A large garage with arched doorways and a caretaker's apartment were added to the house in the 1930s, but otherwise the property appears to have undergone few alterations. The first owner, Franklin Groves, was part of a remarkable family of builders. Along with his father, S. J. Groves, and two brothers, he formed a company in 1908 that specialized in excavating basements. Under Franklin Groves's leadership, the company eventually grew into one of the nation's largest construction firms, with projects all around the world.

J. K. Shaw House

8 J. K. Shaw House

4861 Lake Harriet Blvd. East

Frederick Mann, 1928

A full-dress exercise in Tudor Revival that rambles handsomely across its outsized corner lot. Its designer, Frederick Mann, was the first head of the University of Minnesota's School of Architecture, serving in that position from 1913 until 1936. Mann designed another large house at 4501 Lake Harriet Pkwy. East.

4855 Lake Harriet Pkwy. East

9 House

4855 Lake Harriet Pkwy. East

Charles R. Stinson Architects, 2002

Stinson has made a career out of designs that draw on Frank Lloyd Wright's Prairie Style as well as on the so-called International Style of the 1920s and '30s. By now, he's settled so comfortably into what might be called the Stinson Style that his houses are instantly recognizable.

10 House

4649 Lake Harriet Pkwy. East

Carl J. Bard, 1926

Georgian Revival in yellow and gray limestone.

M. C. Madsen House

11 M. C. Madsen House

4637 Lake Harriet Pkwy. East

Albert Van Dyck, 1923 / enlarged and remodeled, ca. 1990s

The smooth stucco surfaces, blocky massing, and generally sparse ornament of the Spanish Revival houses of the 1920s often gave them a protomodern appearance. That's the case here, where a modern-era addition blends in beautifully with the original portion of the house. The property is adorned with several sculptures, including globes mounted on red pedestals next to steps at the sidewalk.

12 Terrance McCosker House

4615 Lake Harriet Blvd. East

Purcell and Feick, 1909

One of William Purcell's early Craftsman-Prairie houses, quite straightforward, with a gabled roof and banded windows on the second floor. Within, Purcell created an open-floor plan modeled on Frank Lloyd Wright's design for "A Fireproof House for $5,000," published in 1907 in the *Ladies' Home Journal.* Originally clad in wood siding and shingles, the house has been modified over the years in ways that have not enhanced its appearance.

Rufus R. Rand House

13 Rufus R. Rand House

4551 Lake Harriet Pkwy. East

Ernest Kennedy, 1916 / remodeled, ca. 1990s and later

A rather severe Beaux-Arts mansion with a concave curve at the corner, where classically derived ornament frames the front door. The house was originally clad in stone but has since been stuccoed over. The home was designed for members of the Rand family, who owned the Minneapolis Gas Co. Rufus Rand, Jr., a World War I aviator and longtime flight enthusiast, later built the Rand Tower (1929) in downtown Minneapolis.

14 House

4427 Lake Harriet Pkwy. East

D. C. Bennett, 1923

This Spanish-Mediterranean concoction, posed atop a high lot, includes balustraded terraces.

15 William Kenyon House

4301 Lake Harriet Pkwy. East

Kenyon and Maine, 1920

A tall Period Revival house in the Spanish mode. Note the many fine details, such as the lantern that hangs beneath its own tiny roof near the front door.

POI B William Berry Park, Lyndale Park, and Rose Garden

William Berry Park, Berry Dr. and Richfield Rd.

Minneapolis Park Board, 1890 and later

Lyndale Park, including **Rose Garden** and **Peace Garden,** 42nd St. West and Dupont Ave. South (Kings Hwy.)

Minneapolis Park Board, 1891, 1908, 1929, 1983, and later

The more than 100 acres of parkland and gardens between Lake Harriet and Lake Calhoun were acquired in 1890 and 1891. The western portion, originally known as Interlachen Park, was renamed in 1916 in honor of William Berry, the city park system's first superintendent. Lyndale Park, to the east, is best known for its rose garden, begun in 1907 by another park superintendent, Theodore Wirth. It's the second-oldest municipal rose garden in the United States (Wirth also designed the first, in Hartford, CT, in 1903). The park includes two perennial gardens as well.

What's now the peace garden began as a rock garden in 1929. Hard to maintain, the garden was later abandoned and all but forgotten, only to be unearthed by, of all things, a tornado that tore through the park in 1981. Rebuilt over the next 20 years, the garden was dedicated as the Lyndale Park Peace Garden in 1998. Along its pathways you'll find, among other artifacts, stones from the sites of the atomic blasts that devastated Hiroshima and Nagasaki, Japan, in 1945. Lyndale Park is also home to the Roberts Bird Sanctuary. Established in 1947, the sanctuary is named after Thomas S. Roberts, a physician and ornithologist whose 840-page opus, *The Birds of Minnesota* (first published in 1932), is still considered definitive.

16 Interlachen Bridge N

William Berry Dr. over streetcar tracks

William S. Hewett (builder), 1900

Looking at this small bridge, which at first appears to be in the form of a traditional stone arch, you might wonder why it's listed on the National Register of Historic Places. The reason has to do with its structure. The bridge is actually made of reinforced concrete (the stone is a veneer), using a system patented in 1894 by a Swiss engineer, and it's the oldest concrete bridge in Minnesota.

POI C Como-Harriet Streetcar Line and Trolley N L

Between Lakes Harriet and Calhoun

Twin City Rapid Transit Co., 1891 and later / track restored, Minnesota Transportation Museum, 1971–77

Rail operations here date to 1880, when the Motor Line was established on a scenic private right-of-way between Lake Calhoun and Lake Harriet. Electric streetcars replaced the old steam-powered trains in 1891. Seven years later, the route was expanded to become the Como-Harriet interurban line, which extended all the way from suburban Hopkins (with connections to Lake Minnetonka) to downtown St. Paul. The line was the last in the Twin Cities to be abandoned in 1954, when buses replaced all trolley service.

Beginning in 1971, the Minnesota Transportation Museum rebuilt what is now a mile-long segment of track, much of it following the historic right-of-way between 36th St. West at Lake Calhoun and 43rd St. West on the west side of Lake Harriet. In 1989 museum members also built a replica of the original Linden Hills streetcar station at 42nd St. and Queen Ave. South. During summer months, the Minnesota Streetcar Museum (an offshoot of the Transportation Museum) operates two historic wooden streetcars—built by the Twin City Rapid Transit Co. in 1908 and 1915—along the restored track. The track and the older of the two streetcars were added to the National Register of Historic Places in 1977.

17 Lakewood Cemetery

36th St. West and Hennepin Ave.

Charles W. Folsom, Adolph Strauch, and R. M. Copeland, 1871 and later

In 1871 William King proposed the establishment of a large cemetery well away from what he called "the encroachments of the city." Other local nabobs were drafted to help with the planning, and before long a search committee agreed to purchase 130 acres of rolling land between Lakes Calhoun and Harriet for $21,000. The seller of this prime property, conveniently enough, was King himself.

Fifteen of Minneapolis's leading businessmen then banded together to form what was initially known as the Lyndale Cemetery Association but was soon renamed Lakewood. By this time, so-called garden or rural cemeteries, as opposed to crowded old church burial grounds, had become fashionable in the United States. Hoping to create a parklike setting for their new cemetery, which included a pond, Lakewood's trustees hired a team that included Charles W. Folsom, Adolph Strauch, and R. M. Copeland to design the grounds. Folsom was superintendent of Mount Auburn Cemetery in Cambridge, MA, while the Prussian-born Strauch was well known at the time for his role in the design of Cincinnati's Spring Grove Cemetery (1844), which he conceived of as a large open park dotted with graves. Strauch's plan for Spring Grove was so controversial that he received death threats, although his design was ultimately applauded.

With its winding roadways, open vistas, and carefully crafted "natural" look, Lakewood remains the Twin Cities' best example of

Lakewood Cemetery

the Victorian cemetery-park. It's also chock-full of monuments and mausoleums built by prominent Minneapolis families from the Pillsburys to the Dunwoodys. Here, too, are the graves of Civil War soldiers, settlers killed in the U.S.–Dakota War of 1862, prominent members of Minneapolis's early Chinese community, and such political leaders as Floyd B. Olson, Hubert Humphrey, and Paul Wellstone. Other notables buried here include Frank C. Mars, credited with creating the Milky Way candy bar; George Mikan, star center of the old Minneapolis Lakers basketball team; and the ineffable Herbert Khaury, better known by his stage name of Tiny Tim. The cemetery also contains one outstanding work of architecture—the chapel—as well as an administration building and a combined mausoleum-columbarium.

a Administration Building

Near cemetery entrance off 36th St. West

Ernest Kennedy, 1930 / renovated, 1970s, 1992

A dignified Classical Revival building with an inset porch behind an Ionic colonnade.

LOST 2 *The administration building replaced a Romanesque Revival **gatehouse** built at the cemetery's entrance in 1888. The red granite building, demolished in 1930, included checkerboard stonework, a small tower, and a wide, arched gateway. Also gone is a small stone*

comfort station built in 1906 and located by a streetcar stop on the western side of the cemetery. The station, staffed by a female attendant, was a place where women could "freshen up" before visiting the cemetery.

Lakewood Cemetery Memorial Chapel

b Lakewood Cemetery Memorial Chapel ! N i

Near cemetery entrance off 36th St. West

Harry Jones, 1910 (interior by Charles Lamb, New York) / renovated, 1987 / restored, Brooks Borge Skiles (Jim Miller), 1998

This extraordinary building contains one of the nation's finest examples of mosaic art. Constructed at a cost of $150,000 in 1910, it would be hard to duplicate at any price today.

Lakewood Cemetery Memorial Chapel interior

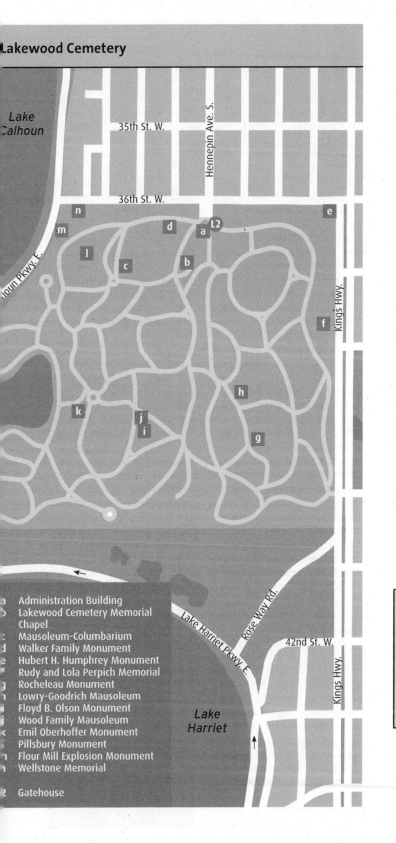

Lakewood Cemetery

Lake Calhoun

35th St. W.

Hennepin Ave. S.

36th St. W.

Calhoun Pkwy. E.

Kings Hwy.

Lake Harriet Pkwy. E.

Rose Way Rd.

42nd St. W.

Kings Hwy.

Lake Harriet

a   Administration Building
b   Lakewood Cemetery Memorial
    Chapel
c   Mausoleum-Columbarium
d   Walker Family Monument
e   Hubert H. Humphrey Monument
f   Rudy and Lola Perpich Memorial
g   Rocheleau Monument
h   Lowry-Goodrich Mausoleum
i   Floyd B. Olson Monument
j   Wood Family Mausoleum
k   Emil Oberhoffer Monument
l   Pillsbury Monument
m   Flour Mill Explosion Monument
n   Wellstone Memorial

2   Gatehouse

Lakewood's board of trustees began considering plans for a new chapel as early as 1904, but it wasn't until 1908 that Harry Jones was hired as the architect. Jones won the commission by proposing a domed stone building modeled on one of the most famous of all churches: Hagia Sophia in Istanbul, built in AD 537 by the Byzantine emperor Justinian I. The chapel's exterior does indeed call Hagia Sophia to mind, albeit on a much smaller scale. Built of St. Cloud granite, the chapel features a 65-foot-high dome rising above a drum ringed with 24 stained-glass windows. These windows serve as a sundial of sorts, indicting the time of day and season based on where light shines in. Four smaller domes rise from the corners of the chapel, which is entered through a pair of ornate bronze doors lodged within a deep arch.

Step inside and you enter a brilliant, shimmering world of tesserae—ten million tiny pieces of marble, colored stone, and glass fused with metal to form mosaics that cover virtually every surface of the interior. Italian artists assembled the mosaics, shipped them on gummed cloth to Minneapolis, and then traveled to the city in the summer of 1909 to install them. Designed by Charles Lamb of New York and his wife, Ella Condie Lamb, the mosaics include 12 Art Nouveau–style angels who circle the dome. Dressed in gowns of various colors, each with its own symbolic significance, the angels are said to represent everything from the 12 tribes of Israel to the 12 apostles of Christ. Another four female figures—representing Love, Faith, Memory, and Hope—adorn the pendentives supporting the dome. Extensive restoration work was performed on the chapel in 1987 and again in 1998, and it remains in excellent condition today. Fittingly enough, Harry Jones's own funeral was held here on September 25, 1935. He was 76 when he died.

c Mausoleum-Columbarium

Near cemetery entrance off 36th St. West

Harley Ellington Corwin and Stirton (Detroit), 1967

A luxuriously appointed building, clad in granite and featuring 24 stained-glass windows designed by the Willet Studios of Philadelphia.

d Walker Family Monument

Near cemetery entrance off 36th St. West

1927

Among those buried here is Thomas Walker, founder of the Walker Art Center.

e Hubert H. Humphrey Monument

Section 51

1978

A simple stone memorial marks the burial place of Minnesota's most famous politician, who served as mayor of Minneapolis, as a longtime U.S. senator, and as vice president of the United States from 1964 to 1968. The memorial's inscription can only be described as Humphreyesque: "I have enjoyed my life, its disappointments outweighed by its pleasure. I have loved my country in a way that some people consider sentimental and out of style. I still do, and I remain an optimist, with joy, without apology, about this country and about the American experiment in democracy."

f Rudy and Lola Perpich Memorial

Section 30

ca. 1995

One of Lakewood's few overtly modernist memorials, consisting of two curving metal shafts. Legendary Iron Range maverick Rudy Perpich served as governor of Minnesota from 1976 to 1979 and from 1983 to 1991. He died in 1995.

g Rocheleau Monument

Section 23

1907

The tallest of Lakewood's monuments, built by Minneapolis businessman Louis Rocheleau in memory of his wife, Charlotte, who died at age 37.

h Lowry-Goodrich Mausoleum

Section 27

1900

A replica of the Parthenon.

i Floyd B. Olson Monument

Section 18

1936

This monument honors Minnesota's first Farmer-Labor Party governor, who died in office at age 44.

j Wood Family Mausoleum

Section 18

1905

An Egyptian Revival–style tomb in the form of a pyramid, set atop one of the cemetery's hills.

k Emil Oberhoffer Monument

Section 44

1933

An obelisk with carved musical notes commemorating the first conductor of the Minneapolis (now Minnesota) Symphony Orchestra.

l Pillsbury Monument

Section 2

1901

A draped female figure stands atop a pedestal in this monument to the milling family. There's also a sheaf of wheat carved into the base.

m Flour Mill Explosion Monument

Section 1-D

1885

Flour Mill Explosion Monument

This obelisk commemorates 18 workers killed in the explosion of the Washburn A Mill in 1878.

n Wellstone Memorial

Section 1-D

2002

U.S. Senator Paul Wellstone and his wife, Sheila, are buried here beside a simple boulder memorial. The Wellstones died in a plane crash in 2002.

Theodore Wirth House–Administration Building

18 Theodore Wirth House–Administration Building N L

3954 Bryant Ave. South

Lowell Lamoreaux, 1910

This house, a Colonial-Mission Revival blend, was the longtime home and office of Theodore Wirth. Born in Switzerland in 1863, Wirth immigrated to the United States in 1888 and later became superintendent of parks in Hartford, CT. Recruited by Charles

Loring, Wirth agreed to come to Minneapolis to head its park system in 1906, but only if the park board would build a residence for him and his family—evidence that executive perks have been around for a long time. The house, built on a portion of William King's old Lyndale Farm, wasn't completed until 1910, and Wirth lived here for the next 36 years.

During Wirth's long tenure in Minneapolis, he supervised dredging and shoreline improvements at city lakes, designed the Lyndale Rose Garden, and added more than 3,000 acres to the city's park system. After his retirement, he wrote a history of the Minneapolis parks. Wirth moved to California in 1946 and died there three years later. He and his wife are buried at nearby Lakewood Cemetery. Still owned by the Minneapolis Park and Recreation Board, the house was added to the National Register of Historic Places in 2002.

Andrew Blauvelt–Scott Winter House

19 Andrew Blauvelt–Scott Winter House

3757 Lyndale Ave. South

Julie Snow Architects, 2008

A stark, minimalist two-story house in concrete and wood. Its most interesting feature is a walled rear courtyard overlooked by floor-to-ceiling windows.

20 Bethlehem Lutheran Church

4100 Lyndale Ave. South

Lang and Raugland, 1927 / later additions

A rugged Gothic Revival church with walls of blue-gray Min-

nesota limestone and a massive square tower.

Kirby Snyder House

21 Kirby Snyder House

4101 Lyndale Ave. South

Kirby T. Snyder, 1915

Although not quite up to the standards of Frank Lloyd Wright or Purcell and Elmslie, this house presents many familiar Prairie elements: bands of casement windows with geometric decorative patterns, overhanging eaves, a low-slung roof, and blocky, asymmetrical massing. Inside, however, the house develops a split personality on the first floor, portions of which feature a variety of deluxe details that are closer in spirit to Beaux-Arts Classicism than the Prairie Style. Snyder, who mainly designed schools and churches during his career, later moved on to California. This is his only known work in Minneapolis.

22 Houses

4203, 4207, 4211, 4219, 4223, 4227, 4231, 4237 Lyndale Ave. South

Irwin Goldstein, 1915–17

These tract houses are all the work of the same architect-builder, who promoted what he called the "Irwin Home Building System." They demonstrate how almost any style could be applied to a basic housing type.

23 House

4355 Lyndale Ave. South

1911

A stucco and brick bungalow with an unusually complex roofline.

24 Church of the Visitation

4530 Lyndale Ave. South

Hills Gilbertson and Hayes, 1948 / addition, 1961 / remodeled, ca. 1970s

In the years after World War II, the St. Paul–Minneapolis Archdiocese established several new parishes to accommodate the swelling population of baby boomers. These new parishes usually began by constructing a combined church-school building. A separate church could be built later as finances permitted. Here, however, a new church never materialized. Sheathed in Mankato-Kasota stone, Visitation is a sturdy, unpretentious building, designed by an architectural firm that specialized in works for the Catholic Church.

25 Knox Presbyterian Church

4747 Lyndale Ave. South

Harry Jones, 1920 / additions, 1954 (new sanctuary), 1959, 1980s

One of the neighborhood's most prominent churches, Gothic Revival in style and built of white stone.

26 House

5152 Lyndale Ave. South

2001

An updated version of the International Style and one of a significant number of modernist houses that lurk amid the historic foliage bordering Minnehaha Creek.

27 Frederick C. Wilhem House

5140 Aldrich Ave. South

S. B. Appleton, 1924

This Spanish-Moorish confection is one of the most charming Period Revival houses in Minneapolis. It features elaborate arabesque ornament enframing the front door, an exceptionally tall and narrow bay window beneath a fanciful copper half dome, and an arcaded side porch

Frederick C. Wilhem House

with twisted columns. Like so much Period Revival architecture, the house conveys a sense of the theatrical and the fantastic, and on a much larger scale you could indeed imagine it as a movie palace, which would be known, of course, as the Alhambra.

Paul Mueller House

28 Paul Mueller Studio and House

studio, 4845 Bryant Ave. South

Purcell Feick and Elmslie, 1911

house, 4844 Aldrich Ave. South

Paul Mueller, 1913

These properties, on high wooded lots, sit back to back. Both were built for Paul Mueller, a landscape architect who came from a wealthy family. After his marriage, Mueller hired Purcell and Elmslie to design a small studio for his new practice. Clad in horizontal board-and-batten siding, the one-story studio isn't one of the firm's major works. Still, it's skillfully done, with a polygonal bay at one end atop a tuck-under garage.

Purcell and Elmslie also planned a house for Mueller, but he ultimately decided to build his own. Although Purcell later dismissed Mueller's design as "ordinary," it is in fact quite unusual. Built of timber framing in the old English manner (not a thing commonly done in 1913), the house is thoroughly Craftsman in spirit. It has vertical board-and-batten siding and rows of casement windows above a rugged base of local limestone punctured by a deep-set entrance arch. Mueller later moved to Chicago; this impressive house remains his sole work of architecture in the Twin Cities.

Charles and Grace Parker House, front terrace

29 House

4750 Colfax Ave. South

Malcolm Rosenstein, 1916

A peculiar variation of the Craftsman foursquare, with wide eaves that sag slightly as though burdened by a heavy weight. Elsewhere, the house shows the influence of the Viennese Secession movement—an early branch of modernism that inspired a handful of early twentieth-century buildings in the Twin Cities.

Charles and Grace Parker House

30 Charles and Grace Parker House ! N Z

4829 Colfax Ave. South

Purcell Feick and Elmslie, 1913

A superb Prairie Style house. The broad gabled roof, carefully grouped windows, side porch, and meticulously worked entry sequence are all classic features of Purcell and Elmslie's work. The entrance, behind a brick-walled terrace that extends across the front of the house, displays one of George Elmslie's finest ornamental designs: a fretsawn arch and frieze above the door. Beams and a pair of pendants extend to either side. Elmslie served for many years as Louis Sullivan's chief draftsman, and the ornament here, with its dazzling combination of geometric and botanical forms, is very Sulli-

vanesque even though it sports Elmslie's signature "V" motif. Elmslie also designed a leaded-glass window in the front door as well as other windows throughout the house. Inside, the house has the usual open plan and includes many built-ins as well as a large brick fireplace.

Charles Parker worked for a wholesale fruit company before becoming co-owner of an auto parts firm. He built this house after he married his partner's daughter, Grace Robertson. The couple stayed in the house for only six years before selling it. The house was added to the National Register of Historic Places in 1992 and has been extensively restored.

31 House

4932 Colfax Ave. South

1914

A very nice Swiss Chalet–style house, with Prairie overtones, rendered in brick and stucco.

32 Harold E. Hineline House

4920 Dupont Ave. South

Purcell Feick and Elmslie, 1910

Purcell and Elmslie always did well by small houses, and this one is no exception. The house is essentially a two-story stucco box, but it's brought to vibrant life by the placement of the windows, the characteristic side porch (originally open), and such lovely details as the sawn-wood ornaments (restored) that project from the small roof above the front entrance. Within, the house has a typical Prairie Style open plan pinwheeling around a central hearth. Not much is known about the first owner, Harold Hineline, other than that he was listed in the 1909 city directory as a bookkeeper.

33 House

5054 Fremont Ave. South

1927

A crisply designed stucco house that appears to have drawn its inspiration from the work of English Arts and Crafts architect Charles Voysey.

Lyman E. Wakefield House

34 Lyman E. Wakefield House *L*

4700 Fremont Ave. South

Purcell Feick and Elmslie, 1912

Architecture is about money and dreams, which do not always make for a perfect match. Like most architects, Purcell and Elmslie struggled to do good work on a limited budget, as was the case here. Lyman Wakefield was a banker and, according to William Purcell, a close man with a dollar. "His interest," Purcell wrote, "was wholly 'how much house for how little money.' From the first we were obliged to make a box of it, and then the struggle began." As it turned out, Purcell and Elmslie produced more than a mere "box" for their banker client. Although the house is indeed quite plain, it displays many deft touches, including a distinctive attic dormer, an upstairs sleeping porch subtly accented by horizontal strips of wood, and a side stair bay with leaded glass. It's not recorded whether Wakefield was happy

with his house, but it would be fair to say he got his money's worth.

James H. McClanahan House

POI D "Lynnhurst" houses

4600 block Fremont Ave. South

Harry Jones and other architects, 1893 and later

Most of the 11 houses along either side of Fremont here date to the 1890s and are thus a decade or more older than homes in the surrounding blocks. This early development stemmed from a plan undertaken in 1893 by Charles Loring, known as the father of the Minneapolis park system but also a promoter and a partner in the Minneapolis Street Railway Co. Loring gave these lots to young married men who worked for him on the condition that they build houses costing at least $3,000. They did just that and named their development—then well out in the country—Lynnhurst. Loring's motives were not entirely philanthropic, since his goal was to jump-start development in the area, which would be good for his business as well as for the streetcar company. His timing was less than ideal, however: the depression of 1893 sank the real estate market, and it would be another decade before additional development worked its way south to Lynnhurst.

At least four of the homes— at 4601, 4626, 4629, and 4639 Fremont—are attributed to Harry Jones. The **John Rickel House,** at 4629, built in 1893, features two hexagonal towers with a chimney rising through one of them. The **James H. McClanahan House,** at 4639, is perhaps the most striking of the lot. Built in 1896, it's a Medieval-Colonial Revival mix that includes an arched front porch and an oddly underscaled front gable.

35 William S. Hewett House

4600 Dupont Ave. South (Kings Hwy.)

Harry Jones, 1906

Although Harry Jones usually designed houses in one historic style or another, many of them were hardly conventional. In this large Georgian Revival home, set sideways on its corner lot so that it faces 46th St., Jones departed from orthodoxy by, among other things, moving the main entry from its usual central position to the far end of the house beside an extended porte cochere. The home's original owner was a prominent engineer who worked with Jones on the Washburn Park Water Tower in the nearby Tangletown neighborhood.

36 House

4344 Dupont Ave. South (Kings Hwy.)

1930

A scenic Norman-Tudor Revival mix that sports an impressive octagonal entry tower, presumably as a last bastion should the peasants ever revolt.

37 House

4320 Dupont Ave. South (Kings Hwy.)

1952

One of the few houses from the 1950s in this neck of the woods, and an early example of the split-level look.

38 Maurice I. Wolf House

4109 Dupont Ave. South (Kings Hwy.)

Purcell Feick and Elmslie, ca. 1912–17

Designed in 1912, this house wasn't built for another five or so years. The final product didn't please William Purcell, who pronounced it "a pretty disappointing build-ing," adding, "If twice as much money could have been spent upon it, I think it might have been quite interesting." The house also suffers from an unwise addition in the form of a widow's walk atop the roof. Be that as it may, the house shows how Purcell and Elmslie, laboring with a tight budget, managed to produce a variant of the usual Craftsman foursquare. They did so by carefully framing the windows, adding some of the firm's characteristic beam-and-pendant ornament, and placing the entrance to one side, as is usually the case with Prairie Style houses. Maurice Wolf, a businessman, supervised construction of the house himself. In the process—at least according to Purcell—he omitted some details specified by the architects.

39 House

4516 Fremont Ave. South

William Channing Whitney, 1910

A foursquare Renaissance Revival house with walls laid up in random blocks of Mankato-Kasota stone. The projecting arched entryway is an unusual feature.

Cyrus Y. Bissell House

40 Cyrus Y. Bissell House

4545 Fremont Ave. South

Cyrus Bissell, 1930

A big scenic sprawl of a house, Tudor-Norman Revival in style, with a round tower rising above the front door. The house's slate roof seems to fall every which way, and the stonework and stucco details are all expertly handled. Bissell, a partner in the successful Minneapolis architectural firm of Haxby Bissell and Stebbins, designed this home for himself and his family. In a 1932 magazine article, Bissell's wife declared: "I've lived in this house for two years now, and as yet I haven't been able to find anything about it that I would want to change."

41 Dr. Charles Wiethoff House

4609 Humboldt Ave. South

Purcell and Elmslie, 1917

One of the last of Purcell and Elmslie's Minneapolis houses, closer in form to a Craftsman chalet—or perhaps even a front-gabled Colonial Revival home—than the typical Prairie Style design. Although the house, clad in cedar siding and stucco, appears quite modest, it has many elegant details such as leaded-glass windows, globed light fixtures, and an arched fireplace—all the work of George Elmslie. The house, built for a physician, includes a flat-roofed garage designed by the architects.

Benjamin Gingold House

42 Benjamin Gingold House

4745 Girard Ave. South

Benjamin Gingold, 1958

A striking but little-known house from the 1950s. Finished in white stucco, the house thrusts forward on its hilly lot with a two-story-high wall of windows extending over a mezzanine and garage. Off to one side, a winding stone staircase leads to the front door, located beside a mysterious round tower that looks a bit like a silo but in fact holds a spiral staircase executed entirely in concrete. The interior is organized around a dramatic living room ringed by balconies. Gingold, who went on to design the 740 River Drive Apartments (1961)

in St. Paul, built the house for himself and his wife. In the 1960s he moved to England, where he spent the rest of his life.

Burroughs Community School

43 Burroughs Community School

1601 50th St. West

Kodet Architectural Group, 2003

Another fine design from the Kodet firm, not quite as powerful as their Whittier School a few miles to the north at 315 26th St. West, but still very convincing. Tall and narrow, this school—which replaced a 1920s-vintage predecessor—consists of two sections, one of which is angled to follow the line of nearby Minnehaha Creek. The lower stories are clad in red brick, with blue green metal above. As with other schools designed by this firm, Burroughs seems to achieve just the right mix of institutional heft—the idea that education is serious and important—and a welcoming presence.

44 Mount Olivet Lutheran Church

5025 Knox Ave. South

Hugo Haeuser (Milwaukee), 1949 / later additions

With 13,000 members, Mount Olivet is the world's largest Lutheran congregation. There were only 20 members when the congregation was founded in 1920, and it was still quite small as late as 1940. However, its population grew rapidly after World War II, leading to the construction of this stone church. Mount Olivet follows English Gothic models and includes a pair of side chapels that can be used for extra seating during services. The long nave, beneath a beamed ceiling, has large stained-glass windows in deep blue and red hues. Mount Olivet also maintains a second church in suburban Victoria.

Floyd B. Olson House

45 Floyd B. Olson House N *L*

1914 49th St. West

1922

This house is listed in the National Register of Historic Places primarily because of its association with Floyd B. Olson, one of Minnesota's most extraordinary politicians. Yet the house, a kind of Classical Revival bungalow with a perfectly symmetrical front facade, is quite interesting. Most bungalows feature Arts and Crafts or Tudor Revival detailing, but here an unlikely pair of classically inspired consoles support an arched roof over the entrance

porch. Olson, who lived here for a good part of his career, is said to have plotted his political strategy in a basement recreation room. A driving force behind the Farmer-Labor Party in Minnesota, Olson won election three times as governor, beginning in 1930. He was poised to run for the U.S. Senate when he died of pancreatic cancer in 1936.

46 House

2006 49th St. West

Architects Small House Service Bureau, 1923

Just after World War I, Minneapolis architect Edwin Brown, then in partnership with Edwin Hewitt, created the Architects Small House Service Bureau. Intended to help alleviate a housing shortage as soldiers returned from overseas, the bureau—which eventually became national in scope—provided architect-designed plans for small, generally inexpensive homes. This brick Colonial Revival house is a representative example of the bureau's work.

6

Linden Hills and Fulton

Linden Hills and Fulton

These two neighborhoods take in the area west of Lake Harriet. Linden Hills extends as far north as Lake Calhoun, while Fulton reaches south to Minnehaha Creek. Both neighborhoods are among the city's most stable and attractive residential precincts, their pleasant streets lined with well-kept, single-family homes.

Parts of Linden Hills, including the so-called Cottage City addition along the southwest side of Lake Calhoun, were platted as early as the 1880s, which was also when the Motor Line route reached Lake Harriet at 42nd Street West and Queen Avenue South. Extensive development didn't begin for another decade, however. A company formed by some of the city's leading real estate men—including Thomas Lowry, William King, and Louis Menage—finally started to attract home builders to Linden Hills in 1894, but only after providing free lots to the first 20 of them.

The majority of homes in Linden Hills date to the early decades of the twentieth century, as do many of the buildings that form a small commercial district around 43rd Street West and Upton Avenue South, where there was once a streetcar loop. Architecture of note here includes the Van Tuyl House (1897), designed by Harry Jones; the delightful Swiss Chalet–style Lovell House (1906); and one of the most mysterious properties in Minneapolis, the Robert and Isabella Giles House (1908), which commands a wooded hilltop and which, like a rare bird, is very hard to spot.

Like Linden Hills, the Fulton neighborhood has a good stock of Period Revival houses built between about 1910 and the early 1930s. Among the best is the Garlick-Magney House (1922) on Washburn Avenue. You'll also find occasional outcroppings of modernist homes from the 1950s and later, especially along Minnehaha Creek. The James Stageberg House (1981) showcases postmodernism. But Fulton's greatest treasure may well be Red Cedar Lane, a glorious little street near Minnehaha Creek, where trees upstage the man-made architecture.

Lake Harriet Spiritual Community

1 Lake Harriet Spiritual Community (Lake Harriet Methodist Episcopal Church)

4401 Upton Ave. South

Fulton and Butler (Uniontown, PA), 1916

A domed Classical Revival church that calls to mind small county courthouses built at this time. Its original occupants, a Methodist congregation, moved to a new church in the 1950s.

2 Bayers Hardware (Harriet Theater)

4312 Upton Ave. South

1911

One of the neighborhood's oldest commercial buildings. Built as a movie theater in 1911, it was converted to a hardware store just seven years later.

POI A Streetcar right-of-way

Parking lot between buildings at 4312 and 4316 Upton Ave. South

The trolleys that once served the Twin Cities almost always ran down streets or through parks. There were, however, a few places where streetcars operated on private rights-of-way in the middle of blocks. This parking lot was once just such a right-of-way.

Tracks here were first built in 1882 by the steam-powered Minneapolis, Lyndale and Minnetonka Railway. From this point, the right-of-way—taken over by streetcars in the 1890s—continued just north of 44th St. West to the city limits and beyond.

3 Church of St. Thomas the Apostle

2914 44th St. West

Joseph V. Vanderbilt, 1927 / additions, 1955, 1996

An Italian Romanesque Revival–style church designed by architect Joseph Vanderbilt, who lived nearby and was a member of the parish. There were originally plans to build a far grander church to the east along Upton Ave., after which this building was to become an auditorium for the adjacent parish school. The Depression and World War II intervened, however, and the new church never materialized.

Frank and Ottalie Fletcher House and garden

LOST 1 *A remarkable home and garden once stood along 44th St. West in what is now the parking lot for St. Thomas Church. The* **Frank and Ottalie Fletcher House** *was built in about 1900 by an insurance agent and his wife. The Arts and Crafts house, which featured a rough boulder base, was notable in its own right, but what really made the property stand out was its elaborate Japanese garden. Under the direction of local decorator and tastemaker John Bradstreet, a gardener named Yamado Baske worked with the Fletchers to create a remarkable outdoor space. The garden included a pond crossed by*

a rustic footbridge, winding pathways, and cedar trees sheltering a Buddha. In 1923 the Fletchers sold their home and garden to St. Thomas. After serving as the parish's rectory, the house was demolished in 1940, and the high-maintenance garden went with it.

4 Linden Hills Community Library N L

2900 43rd St. West

Bard and Vanderbilt, 1931 / restored and enlarged, Leonard Parker Associates, 2002

Although this library's Tudor Revival styling is conventional, inside you'll find a series of gracious reading rooms, including one with a fireplace. The Linden Hills branch is among 14 neighborhood libraries established in Minneapolis between 1894 and 1936. Most were built or acquired under the leadership of Gratia Alta Countryman, longtime head of the city's library system.

2726–32 43rd St. West, detail

5 Commercial building

2726–32 43rd St. West

Downs and Eads, 1915

A Prairie Style commercial building with vigorous terra-cotta ornament in the manner of Louis Sullivan and George Elmslie. It was originally built as a telephone exchange.

6 Cafe Twenty Eight (Fire Station No. 28) N L

2724 43rd St. West

Downs and Eads, 1914 / remodeled, TEA2 Architects, 1994, 1996

A spiffy old fire station, the first built in Minneapolis solely for motorized equipment. It's now been converted to a restaurant.

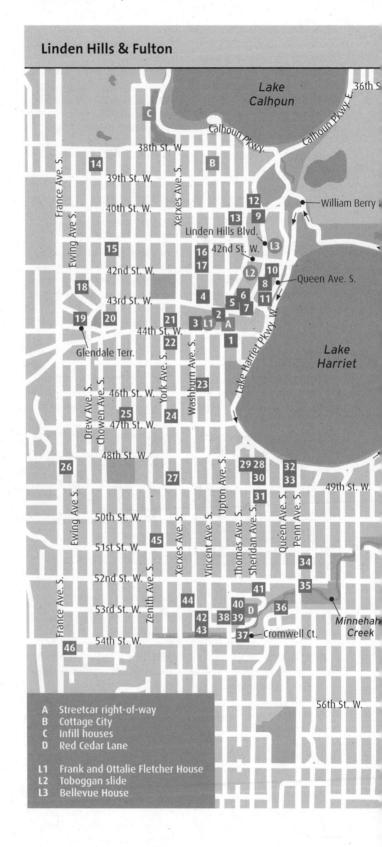

Linden Hills & Fulton

A   Streetcar right-of-way
B   Cottage City
C   Infill houses
D   Red Cedar Lane

L1   Frank and Ottalie Fletcher House
L2   Toboggan slide
L3   Bellevue House

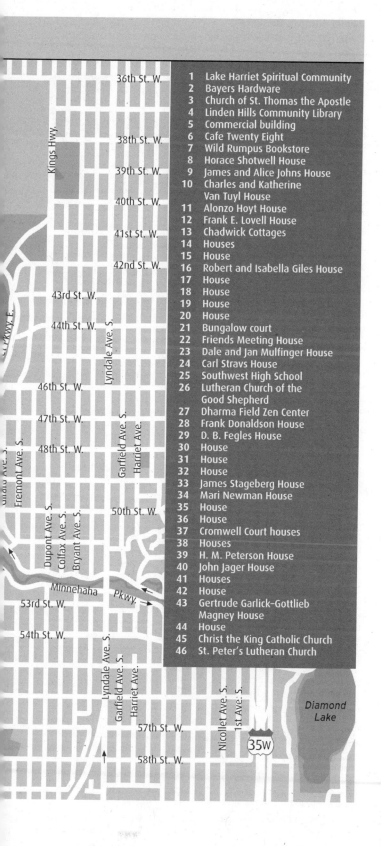

1 Lake Harriet Spiritual Community
2 Bayers Hardware
3 Church of St. Thomas the Apostle
4 Linden Hills Community Library
5 Commercial building
6 Cafe Twenty Eight
7 Wild Rumpus Bookstore
8 Horace Shotwell House
9 James and Alice Johns House
10 Charles and Katherine
   Van Tuyl House
11 Alonzo Hoyt House
12 Frank E. Lovell House
13 Chadwick Cottages
14 Houses
15 House
16 Robert and Isabella Giles House
17 House
18 House
19 House
20 House
21 Bungalow court
22 Friends Meeting House
23 Dale and Jan Mulfinger House
24 Carl Stravs House
25 Southwest High School
26 Lutheran Church of the
   Good Shepherd
27 Dharma Field Zen Center
28 Frank Donaldson House
29 D. B. Fegles House
30 House
31 House
32 House
33 James Stageberg House
34 Mari Newman House
35 House
36 House
37 Cromwell Court houses
38 Houses
39 H. M. Peterson House
40 John Jager House
41 Houses
42 House
43 Gertrude Garlick–Gottlieb
   Magney House
44 House
45 Christ the King Catholic Church
46 St. Peter's Lutheran Church

36th St. W.
38th St. W.
39th St. W.
40th St. W.
41st St. W.
42nd St. W.
43rd St. W.
44th St. W.
46th St. W.
47th St. W.
48th St. W.
50th St. W.
53rd St. W.
54th St. W.
57th St. W.
58th St. W.

Kings Hwy.
Lyndale Ave. S.
Garfield Ave. S.
Harriet Ave.
Fremont Ave. S.
Dupont Ave. S.
Colfax Ave. S.
Bryant Ave. S.
Lyndale Ave. S.
Garfield Ave. S.
Harriet Ave.
Nicollet Ave. S.
1st Ave. S.

Minnehaha   Pkwy.

Diamond
Lake

35W

7 Wild Rumpus Bookstore (Lake Harriet Commercial Club)

2718–20 43rd St. West

Downs and Eads, 1911 / remodeled, Bowers Bryan and Feidt, 1992

This brick Classical Revival building was originally home to a club. The children's bookstore within, designed in 1992, is a delight, featuring many whimsical touches.

8 Horace Shotwell House

4225 Linden Hills Blvd.

1910

Most of the homes along Linden Hills Blvd. are of the two-story variety, but here's a one-story Craftsman interloper pepped up with a shot of Spanish flavoring.

LOST 2 *In about 1915, the Minneapolis Park Board, using wood salvaged from the old City Hall (1873–1912) at Bridge Square, built a long* **toboggan slide** *that began at 42nd St. and Linden Hills Blvd. The slide went all the way down the hill, across the streetcar tracks, and well out onto frozen Lake Harriet. Similar slides were once a common sight in local parks, with some of the largest being constructed for St. Paul winter carnivals. You can only imagine what the liability insurance would cost today.*

LOST 3 *Where a home now stands at 4051 Linden Hills Blvd. was once the site of the* **Bellevue House,** *a lakeside hotel built in 1884. The hotel was taken over in 1894 by the Lurline Boat Club but was being used as a boardinghouse when it burned down in 1901. The home that's here now dates to 1905.*

9 James and Alice Johns House

4000 Linden Hills Blvd.

Orff and Joralemon, 1894

One of the first houses built in this part of Linden Hills, on a lot that the neighborhood's developers provided free of charge. The original owner, with the curiously plural name of James Johns, was in the grain business.

Charles and Katherine Van Tuyl House

10 Charles and Katherine Van Tuyl House

4236 Queen Ave. South

Harry Jones, 1897 and later

Set on a hill above terraced walls, this half-timbered, brick and stucco Tudor Revival mansion was built for Charles Van Tuyl, who was in the insurance business. He and wife Katherine lived next door at 4224 Queen before hiring Harry Jones to design this home on a double lot offering excellent views of Lake Harriet. Later, Van Tuyl acquired two more lots to the rear along Linden Hills Blvd. and created a mini-estate outfitted with stables, a tennis court, and a greenhouse. Van Tuyl and his wife lived here until their deaths (hers in 1929, his a year later).

In 1933 a new owner, U.S. Senator Thomas D. Schall, moved in. A lawyer and a Republican, Schall was also the first blind person elected to the U.S. House of Representatives and, later, to the U.S. Senate. His first senate campaign, against incumbent Magnus Johnson—memorably described by *Time* magazine as a man of "leisurely mental processes"—was conducted with all the dignity you'd expect of a hotly contested political race. A Schall campaign button, for example, offered this pithy slogan: "Schall is blind but Magnus is dumb." Schall, who'd lost his sight in an accident as a young man, had nearly completed his second senate term in late 1935 when he was struck and killed by a car in Washington, DC.

11 Alonzo Hoyt House

4290 Queen Ave. South

Carl Gage, 1910

A pared-down bungalow with little of the Arts and Crafts flavoring you'd expect to find on a house of its type. The round porch columns are unusual. When he built this house, Alonzo Hoyt was president of a brass and iron firm. As a younger man, he'd managed the first pavilion at Lake Harriet from 1888 until it burned down in 1891.

Frank E. Lovell House

12 Frank E. Lovell House

2504 40th St. West

Lowell Lamoreaux, 1906

A wonderful Swiss Chalet–style house. Balconies sheltered under deep overhanging eaves extend all the way around the house, which also has a terrace offering views of Lake Harriet. The original owner, it is said, operated a private kindergarten here for 20 years.

POI B Cottage City

Area bounded by Richfield Rd., Xerxes Ave. South, Calhoun Pkwy. West, and 40th St. West

This area on the south side of Lake Calhoun was platted in 1882–83 by developer Louis Menage as Cottage City. His plat was unusual because it specified lots just 25 feet wide, as opposed to the Minneapolis norm of 40 feet. Menage hoped these small lots would attract people interested in building summer lake cottages. But the sort of quasi-resort community he had in mind developed slowly, and most of the early homes that survive here weren't built until after 1900. As Cottage City filled out, lots were

often combined, but some of the original narrow ones remain, mostly along Thomas, Vincent, and Upton Aves. The old "cottages" themselves are scattered here and there, usually in remodeled form. There's a particularly good collection on the 3800 block of Thomas.

Chadwick Cottages

13 Chadwick Cottages *L*

2617 40th St. West

Loren Chadwick (builder), 1902 / enlarged and combined, 1972

Perhaps the best remaining example of what Cottage City's small homes once looked like. Contractor Loren Chadwick built three identical cottages here in 1902. One was removed in 1929, but the other two stayed put. In 1972 new owners merged the pair into a single home by connecting them with an addition at the rear.

Zenith Ave. house

POI C Infill houses

3600 block Zenith Ave. South

various architects, ca. 2000 and later

This block has several McMansions akin to those found elsewhere around the Minneapolis lakes. In a growing number of cases, these infill homes are the result of teardowns, in which perfectly good houses are demolished to make way for bigger and fancier properties. Like it or not, this phenomenon is hardly new: the first significant wave of teardowns in the Twin Cities occurred in the 1880s, mainly along ritzy streets like Summit Ave. in St. Paul. What's different now is that outsized new houses are often being wedged into modest lots, and the effect is much like squeezing an SUV into a tiny parking space: it can be done, but seldom gracefully.

14 Houses

3800 blocks Chowen and Drew Aves. South

various architects, ca. 1926–32

Welcome to "Tudorland." Tudor Revival tract houses from the late 1920s and early 1930s abound on these blocks. Most of the houses are finished in stucco with brick and stone trim and, in many cases, a bit of ye olde (fake) half-timbering as well.

15 House

4108 Chowen Ave. South

2006

Nostalgic new houses in all manner of historic styles are common in the Lake District, but this one is a real oddity, offering an updated take on the Italianate style of the 1860s and 1870s, complete with bracketed eaves.

Robert and Isabella Giles House

16 Robert and Isabella Giles House

4106 Vincent Ave. South

Jager and Stravs, 1908

If you didn't know this house existed, the odds are you would never notice it—in the summer months, at least—even if you walked right past along Vincent Ave. or 41st St. West. The house occupies an exceptional site—a wooded hill hidden away within the depths of an otherwise ordi-

nary residential block—and it does nothing to advertise its presence. Its architects, John Jager and Carl Stravs, were born in the Austro-Hungarian Empire and were trained by leaders of the Viennese Secessionist movement, an early fork along the road to modernism. They were also influenced by the Prairie School work of Frank Lloyd Wright and his followers. This house has something of a Prairie look, but its curving eaves, blue brick accents, and exotic Art Nouveau details make it a one-of-a-kind production. It was built for Robert Tait Giles, an artist who founded his own stained-glass company in Minneapolis, and his wife, Isabella. The couple eventually moved to Chicago, where some of Giles's best work can be found.

17 House

2912 42nd St. West

1912 and later

Houses subjected to what might be called artistic interventions are not unheard of in Linden Hills, and here's an example: an early twentieth-century Arts and Crafts home that's been jazzed up with a rather startling, angular door surround.

4221 Ewing Ave. South

18 House

4221 Ewing Ave. South

Alchemy Architects, 2007

The Alchemy firm developed a small modular structure called the "weeHouse" in 2003. Here, the architects tied together four of their boxlike modules to create a two-story, 2,200-square-foot residence. At that size, the house isn't exactly "wee," but it is highly energy efficient and fits in quite nicely with its Arts and Crafts and Period Revival neighbors.

19 House

3714 Glendale Terr.

1912

A severe white stucco box, Spanish Revival in inspiration, with an arcaded front porch and little if any ornament. The house bears at least some resemblance to the contemporaneous work of San Diego architect Irving Gill, who boiled down the various California Spanish styles into something approaching modernism.

20 House

3514 Motor Pl.

ca. 1890

Motor Pl. takes its name from the Motor Line railroad (later converted to streetcar use) that once ran just to the south along its route between downtown Minneapolis and Lake Minnetonka. This festively painted Victorian was moved here.

3110–12 44th St. West

21 Bungalow court

3110–12 44th St. West

1929

Consisting of six units, this is one of the largest and last bungalow courts from the 1920s in the Twin Cities.

22 Friends Meeting House (St. Thomas the Apostle Catholic Church)

4401 York Ave. South

Edward J. Donahue, 1908–9 / renovated, Close Associates (Gar Hargens), 1990

A calm, simple little building, domestic in scale, and just what you'd expect of a Quaker meeting house.

23 Dale and Jan Mulfinger House

4529 Washburn Ave. South

Dale Mulfinger, 1996

Architect Dale Mulfinger and his firm have specialized in designing houses, often quite compact, that evoke the warm, woodsy feel of the Arts and Crafts era. This house, deep red in color, is long and narrow, with a front-facing gable and vertical board-and-batten siding.

24 Carl Stravs House

4649 York Ave. South

Carl B. Stravs, 1929

This cubic, shingle-clad house built by and for architect Carl Stravs doesn't jump out at you but does offer one unusual feature: an angular split window that follows the line of the staircase inside. It's similar to a window at the Phi Gamma Delta fraternity house Stravs designed at the University of Minnesota in 1911.

25 Southwest High School

3414 47th St. West

Bureau of Buildings (Edward Enger, supervising architect) with Lang and Raugland, 1940 / additions, 1942, 1956, 1968

The last high school built in Minneapolis before World War II. The style is Moderne but not strongly so.

26 Lutheran Church of the Good Shepherd

4801 France Ave. South (or 4800 Ewing Ave. South)

Hills Gilbertson and Hayes, 1950 / Art: relief sculpture (front of church), 1950

An early modernist church in the brick box mode. The building is quite stark except for some stained glass and a huge relief sculpture of a shepherd and lamb that's pinned to the front facade.

One of the architects, Victor Gilbertson, had worked with Eliel Saarinen on Christ Lutheran

Lutheran Church of the Good Shepherd

Church in the Longfellow neighborhood of Minneapolis just a year or so earlier, and the influence of that seminal design is clearly evident here. An education wing extends to the south side of the church and encloses a courtyard.

27 Dharma Field Zen Center (St. Andrew's Lutheran Church) *L*

3118 49th St. West

Downs and Eads, 1907

A small Arts and Crafts church building designed to resemble a house. Originally located at 44th St. West and Upton Ave. South, the building was constructed in 1907 for a Methodist congregation but was sold in 1916 to St. Andrew's Lutheran Church and moved here. It has been used as a Zen center since 1997.

Frank Donaldson House

28 Frank Donaldson House

4807 Sheridan Ave. South

Stebbins Haxby and Bissell, 1931

Just uphill from Lake Harriet, this large stone house has a Tudor arch at the front door but few other Tudor Revival details. Overall, it evokes the quietly picturesque work of English Arts and Crafts architects such as Charles Voysey, and it's very nicely done.

29 D. B. Fegles House

4816 Sheridan Ave. South

Dorr and Dorr, 1922

This Craftsman-Prairie blend is similar to some of Purcell and Elmslie's houses but lacks the exquisite detailing that makes their best designs so memorable.

30 House

4831 Sheridan Ave. South

Louis Bersback, 1927

A Period Revival house that hovers, like a piece of atonal music, somewhere between the usual stylistic keys. The projecting entrance, with its oversized brick quoins and split pediment, has a kind of baroque bravado, but other details suggest everything from French Provincial to Tudor Revival.

31 House

4901 Sheridan Ave. South

1960

A flat-roofed concrete block house set behind a small courtyard and a garage that projects out toward the street.

32 House

4815 Queen Ave. South

1907

A bungalow with a chalet-style balcony and an inset screened porch.

James Stageberg House

33 James Stageberg House

4820 Penn Ave. South

James Stageberg, 1981

Built by the architect as his own residence, this fanciful green and purple house is one of the more colorful specimens from the postmodern era in the Twin Cities. It includes a rooftop porch and an observation deck.

Mari Newman House

34 Mari Newman House

5117 Penn Ave. South

1915 / renovated, Mari Newman, ca. 1988 and later

Architecture and art merge in this eccentric folk house. Self-taught artist Mari Newman grew up in the house—a standard bungalow—and in the 1980s began to transform it according to a highly personal vision. Her boldest gesture was to paint the house in an array of colors—red, blue, green, purple, brown, orange, and yellow being among the selected hues—and then decorate it with fields of flowers and circles, which she calls "patterned abstracts." The unorthodox treatment continues on the roof, which is shingled in a striped pattern. A revolving collection of art objects—generally of the "found" variety—adorns the front yard.

35 House

2205 52nd St. West

Carl B. Stravs, 1923 / addition, Albertsson Hansen Architecture, ca. 2006

A saltbox cottage with its gable end facing the street and its windows arranged in a rather peculiar way. The rear addition, faced in red board-and-batten siding, offers views of Minnehaha Creek.

36 House

2328 53rd St. West

James Stageberg, 1968

A wood-sided International Style house. Several other high-quality,

modernist houses are located along this side of 53rd St.

37 Cromwell Court houses

2602, 2604, 2606, 2808 Cromwell Ct.

Carl Graffunder (2604 and 2606) and Stowell Leach (2808), 1951–52

Another of Minnehaha Creek's early modernist enclaves. The most interesting house, at 2602, consists of two flat-roofed volumes (house and garage) connected by a breezeway.

38 Houses

5309, 5312, 5315, 5319 Upton Ave. South

Purcell and Strauel, 1929–33

These four speculative houses were designed by William Purcell, living at the time in Portland, OR, and minus his old partner, George Elmslie. By the late 1920s, the Prairie Style was no longer in vogue, so Purcell—working with one of his former draftsman, Frederick Strauel—had to dress his designs in Period Revival attire. Even so, he couldn't quite shed his Prairie roots, which are particularly evident in the house at 5315 Upton. Its second-story windows are arranged in a band under the eaves (a Prairie hallmark), while the arched entrance looks to have been drawn from one of Purcell and Elmslie's small-town banks.

POI D Red Cedar Lane

Off Upton Ave. South between 52nd and 53rd Sts.

John Jager, 1904 and later

It would be hard to find a more beautiful street in the Twin Cities than this short, narrow cul-de-sac created over a century ago on a hillside above Minnehaha Creek. The man behind it was John Jager, who was born in what is today Slovenia and educated in Vienna before emigrating to Minneapolis in 1902. A highly skilled planner and architect, Jager also built his own house here. The plantings along the street include not only red cedars but also, behind

Red Cedar Lane

them, rows of towering white pines. When you see how gorgeous these evergreens look year-round, you wonder why more such streets weren't planned in the Twin Cities, where winter—even in the age of global warming—is always the longest season.

H. M. Peterson House

39 H. M. Peterson House

3 Red Cedar Ln.

William Purcell, 1928

A variant of the English Cottage type and one of the more interesting designs from what might be called Purcell's post-Prairie years. The house's wood-shake roof curls up like a wave over the front door, which features a surprising pointed arch. A lower level not visible from the street is built into a hill facing Minnehaha Creek. The first owner was a real estate developer who also commissioned Purcell to design nine speculative houses nearby, including four on Russell Ave.

40 John Jager House

6 Red Cedar Ln.

John Jager, 1904 / later additions and renovations

As designed and built by John Jager, this was a rather spartan house rising from a wide boulder base to a smaller second floor with an open, south-facing porch. Over the years the house has been enlarged, stuccoed over on its upper floors, and otherwise modified. Jager, who lived here until his death in 1959, had a varied career. He designed the superb St. Bernard's Church in St. Paul (1906), prepared a 1905 city plan for Minneapolis, worked as an engineer for the architectural firm of Hewitt and Brown, and later organized and maintained a vast archives, now at the University of Minnesota, documenting the work of William Purcell and George Elmslie. Despite his achievements, Jager died a bitter man, believing his work had never been properly appreciated.

41 Houses

10, 16, 20, 30 Russell Ct.

various architects, 1951–65

One of several outposts of post–World War II modernist architecture along Minnehaha Creek. The four houses here are quite understated, and for the most part they've aged well. The most interesting house—at 30 Russell Ct., built in 1953 and designed by Benjamin Gingold—steps downhill to the creek and has a secluded rear terrace.

42 House

5312 Vincent Ave. South

Purcell and Strauel, 1928

Another "spec" house designed by William Purcell and his former draftsman. Here the style is Colonial Revival, albeit of a very abstract, chaste kind.

Gertrude Garlick–Gottlieb Magney House

43 Gertrude Garlick– Gottlieb Magney House

5329 Washburn Ave. South

Magney and Tusler, 1922

From the front, this charming if rather sedate English Cottage–style house doesn't appear exceptional. Walk around to the back (off Brookwood Terr.), however, and you'll find a series of brick garden walls that include a round gazebo with a conical roof. Resembling a miniature castle, the gazebo adds a note of romance to the architectural proceedings. As it turns out, romance was also in the air. The house was built for Gertrude Garlick, who worked for the Young Quinlan Co., a fashionable clothing store in downtown Minneapolis. The architect was Gottlieb Magney, whose firm would soon design a new store building for Young Quinlan (1926) and, later, the Foshay Tower (1929). Two years after this house was completed, Garlick and Magney were married.

44 House

5250 Washburn Ave. South

1912 and later

This house, set far back on its lot, looks to have undergone quite a few remodelings and additions. But the real eye-catcher here—best seen from the alley—is a fantastic chimney made from bricks, stone, pipes, ducts, metal rings, a metal ladder, chains, cinder blocks, sewer tiles, and numerous other scrap materials.

45 Christ the King Catholic Church

5029 Zenith Ave. South

Hills Gilbertson and Hayes, 1958 / later additions

A late, stripped-down example of the Gothic Revival style. Like many Twin Cities churches from the 1950s, it's faced in Mankato-Kasota stone.

St. Peter's Lutheran Church

46 St. Peter's Lutheran Church

5421 France Ave. South

Ralph Rapson, 1956

Located a half block outside the Minneapolis city limits in Edina, this church in the round (actually, it's an octagon) is one of Rapson's typically energetic works, featuring steep gables with triangular windows that burst out from their base like flower petals. Inside, a star-shaped ceiling focuses the worship space above a central altar. Most new churches these days are far more tame—and far less interesting—than what Rapson produced here.

Annotated Bibliography

Adams, John S., and Barbara J. VanDrasek. *Minneapolis–St. Paul: People, Place and Public Life.* Minneapolis: University of Minnesota Press, 1993. Written by two geographers, this book provides a useful overview of the growth and development of the Twin Cities.

Atwater, Isaac, ed. *History of the City of Minneapolis, Minnesota.* New York: Munsell and Co., 1893. A big subscription book of the kind popular in the nineteenth century. It offers intriguing sketches of the city's white, overwhelmingly Protestant, and exclusively male establishment.

Besse, Kirk. *Show Houses, Twin Cities Style.* Minneapolis: Victoria Publications, 1997. A history of St. Paul and Minneapolis movie theaters.

Borchert, John R., David Gebhard, David Lanegran, and Judith A. Martin. *Legacy of Minneapolis: Preservation amid Change.* Minneapolis: Voyageur Press, 1983. A rather disorganized book that nonetheless contains much interesting information about the city's architecture and history.

Bromley, Edward A. *Minneapolis Portrait of the Past.* 1890. Reprint, Minneapolis: Voyageur Press, 1973. Wonderful photographs showing the city's earliest days.

Brooks, H. Allen. *The Prairie School: Frank Lloyd Wright and His Midwest Contemporaries.* 1972. Reprints, New York: Norton, 1976, 2006. Still the best survey of the Prairie School, with much information about its chief Minnesota practitioners, William Purcell and George Elmslie.

Conforti, Michael, ed. *Art and Life on the Upper Mississippi, 1890–1915: Minnesota 1900.* Newark: University of Delaware Press, 1994. Includes chapters on turn-of-the-century Minnesota architecture and a long essay on the work of Purcell and Elmslie.

Diers, John W., and Aaron Isaacs. *Twin Cities by Trolley: The Streetcar Era in Minneapolis and St. Paul.* Minneapolis: University of Minnesota Press, 2007. The fullest account available of the streetcar system that helped shape the Lake District and almost every other neighborhood in the Twin Cities.

Down at the Lake: A Historical Portrait of Linden Hills and the Lake Harriet District. Minneapolis: Linden Hills History Study Group, 2001. A solid neighborhood history.

Flanagan, Barbara. *Minneapolis.* New York: St. Martin's Press, 1973. The longtime newspaper columnist provides a breezy tour of her beloved Minneapolis. Fun to read, but don't rely on it for history lessons.

Gardner, John S., ed. *The Midwest in American Architecture.* Chicago: University of Illinois Press, 1991. Includes a long chapter on George Elmslie and his work in Minnesota and elsewhere.

Gebhard, David. *Purcell & Elmslie: Prairie Progressive Architects.* Patricia Gebhard, ed. Layton, UT: Gibbs Smith, 2006. An analysis of the architects' work by a pioneering scholar in the field.

Gebhard, David, and Tom Martinson. *A Guide to the Architecture of Minnesota.* Minneapolis: University of Minnesota Press, 1977. Now badly dated, this remains the only comprehensive guide of its kind. The chapters on the Twin Cities omit many significant buildings, especially in St. Paul.

Hession, Jane King, Rip Rapson, and Bruce N. Wright. *Ralph Rapson: Sixty Years of Modern Design.* Afton, MN: Afton Historical Society Press, 1999. A look at the life and work of Minnesota's best-known modern architect.

Hudson, Horace B., ed. *A Half Century in Minneapolis.* Minneapolis: Hudson Publishing Co., 1908. Yet another compilation, with some interesting stuff lurking amid the standard salutes to wealth and progress.

Kenney, Dave. *Twin Cities Album: A Visual History.* St. Paul: Minnesota Historical Society Press, 2005. A nice array of photographs and other images that provide an overview of the history of Minneapolis and St. Paul. There's also an informative text.

Kudalis, Eric, ed. *100 Places Plus 1: An Unofficial Architectural Survey of Favorite Minnesota Sites.* Minneapolis: AIA Minnesota, 1996. Various essayists describe their favorite buildings and places in Minnesota.

Lanegran, David, and Ernest Sandeen. *The Lake District of Minneapolis: A History of the Calhoun-Isles Community.* St. Paul: Living Historical Museum, 1979. The only formal history of the Lake District. The book, which offers a survey of the district's architecture, includes suggested walking tours.

Legler, Dixie, and Christian Korab. *At Home on the Prairie: The Houses of Purcell and Elmslie.* San Francisco, CA: Chronicle Books, 2006. A survey of the firm's domestic work, illustrated with outstanding photographs.

McAlester, Virginia, and Lee McAlester. *A Field Guide to American Houses.* New York: Alfred A. Knopf, 1984. Obviously this isn't a work about the Twin Cities, but it is a superb guidebook, with excellent drawings and photographs to help you identify the style of almost any kind of house.

Martin, Judith, and David Lanegran. *Where We Live: The Residential Districts of Minneapolis and Saint Paul.* Minneapolis: University of Minnesota Press, 1983. Lots of good information about neighborhoods in the Twin Cities.

Millett, Larry. *AIA Guide to the Twin Cities: The Essential Source on the Architecture of Minneapolis and St. Paul.* St. Paul: Minnesota Historical Society Press, 2007. Includes chapters on the Lake District and surrounding neighborhoods.

———. *The Curve of the Arch: The Story of Louis Sullivan's Owatonna Bank.* St. Paul: Minnesota Historical Society Press, 1985. Includes a biographical sketch of George Elmslie.

Millett, Larry (with photographs by Jerry Mathiason). *Twin Cities Then and Now.* St. Paul: Minnesota Historical Society Press, 1996. Historic photographs of more than 70 street scenes paired with new pictures taken from the same locations, including two from the Lake District.

Nord, Mary Ann, comp. *The National Register of Historic Places in Minnesota.* St. Paul: Minnesota Historical Society Press, 2003. Lists every Minnesota building on the register.

Olivarez, Jennifer Komar. *Progressive Design in the Midwest: The Purcell-Cutts House and the Prairie School Collection at the Minneapolis Institute of Arts.* Minneapolis: University of Minnesota Press, 2000. A richly illustrated history of Purcell and Elmslie's most famous house.

Olson, Russell L. *The Electric Railways of Minnesota.* Hopkins: Minnesota Transportation Museum, 1977. Written by a trolley buff, this study describes in sometimes numbing detail the Twin Cities' late, great streetcar system.

Poppeliers, John C., S. Allen Chambers, Jr., and Nancy B. Schwartz. *What Style Is It? A Guide to American Architecture.* 1983. Rev. ed., Washington, DC: Preservation Press, ca. 2002. A useful guidebook that includes photographs, drawings, a glossary of terms, and a good bibliography.

Prairie School Architecture in Minnesota, Iowa, Wisconsin. St. Paul: Minnesota Museum of Art, 1982. Six essays on Prairie School architecture, lavishly illustrated with photographs and drawings.

Schmid, Calvin F. *Social Saga of Two Cities: An Ecological and Statistical Study of Social Trends in Minneapolis and St. Paul.* Minneapolis: Council of Social Agencies, Bureau of Social Research, 1937. Conceived as a Depression-era project, this is one of the most informative books ever written about the Twin Cities. Especially valuable are the superb maps and charts.

Shutter, Marion D., ed. *History of Minneapolis, Gateway to the Northwest.* 3 vols. Chicago and Minneapolis: S. J. Clarke Publishing Co., 1923. This plump compendium, best taken in small doses, provides useful information about the city's early movers and shakers.

Stevens, John H. *Personal Recollections of Minnesota and Its People, and Early History of Minneapolis.* Minneapolis: Privately published, 1890. Stevens, who was among the first residents of Minneapolis, laid out the downtown street grid still in use today.

Stipanovich, Joseph. *City of Lakes: An Illustrated History of Minneapolis.* Woodland Hills, CA: Windsor Publications, 1982. The most recent full-dress history of the city and on the whole well done. Includes many photographs.

Torbert, Donald R. *Minneapolis Architecture and Architects, 1848–1908: A Study of Style Trends in Architecture in a Midwestern City Together with a Catalogue of Representative Buildings.* PhD diss., University of Minnesota, 1951. A good source of information about early Minneapolis architects.

———. *Significant Architecture in the History of Minneapolis.* Minneapolis: City Planning Commission, 1969. Torbert did pioneering research in local architectural history, but an extreme modernist bias often clouded his judgment.

Vandam, Elizabeth A. *Harry Wild Jones: American Architect.* Minneapolis: Nodin Press, 2008. A good survey of the work of Harry Jones, who designed many homes, churches, and park buildings in the Lake District.

Writers' Program, Works Progress Administration. *Minneapolis: The Story of a City.* 1940. New York: AMS Press, 1948. A typical product of the Federal Writers Program sponsored by the Works Progress Administration.

Index

Every building and site described in the Guide is listed as a primary entry in the index, both by previous and current names. Building and street names beginning with numbers are alphabetized as if spelled out. The names of people, firms, organizations, and government offices involved in creating the works listed in the Guide appear in UPPER AND LOWER CASE SMALL CAPS. Unless otherwise indicated, they are architects, associated artists, or builders. Names of geographic areas or communities appear in **_boldface italic_**. A page reference in **boldface** indicates a photograph of the building, area, or other work.

The following abbreviations appear in the index:

Admin.	Administration	Co.	Company	MN	Minnesota
Amer.	American	Condos.	Condominiums	Mpls.	Minneapolis
Apts.	Apartments	Corp.	Corporation	Natl.	National
Assocs.	Associates	Ct.	Court	Pkwy.	Parkway
Bldg.	Building	Dr.	Drive	RR	Railroad/Railway
Blvd.	Boulevard	H.S.	High School	St.	Street
Cem.	Cemetery	Ins.	Insurance		

Picture Credits

Diane D. Brown: 14 right, 15 left and bottom right, 21 left, 28 top, 30 left, 32 right, 38 left, 39 left, 42 top left, 43 right, 44, 47 left and right, 49 left, 56 right, 61, 64 bottom left, 69 bottom, 73 bottom right, 76 top right, 80 right, 82 left, 83 left, 85 left

David Enblom: 73 top left and top right, 79 top, 81 top and bottom, 85 right, 89 right, 93 left

Brian M. Gardner: 76 bottom right

Bill Jolitz: 9 top and bottom, 14 top left, 17 right, 18 left and right, 19 left and right, 20 top and bottom, 21 top and bottom right, 22 left, 29 top and bottom left, 31, 33, 34 left and right, 35 top and bottom, 38 right, 39 right, 43 left, 48 left and bottom right, 49 right, 53 top and bottom, 56 left, 57, 58 left and top right, 59, 60 left and right, 62 top and bottom left and right, 64 top left and right, 69 top, 72 right, 73 bottom left, 74, 76 top, 79 bottom, 80 left, 83 right, 84, 86, 88, 92, 93 top and bottom right, 94 left and right, 95, 96 top and bottom left and right, 97, 98 top and left, 99 left and right

Frank Mazzocco: 25 top and bottom left, 28 bottom, 30 right, 32 left, 42 bottom left and right, 45, 46

Minneapolis Institute of Arts, Bequest of Anson Cutts, Jr.: 29 right

Minnesota Historical Society: 12 left and right, 13 top and bottom, 14 bottom left, 15 top right, 16, 17 left, 22 right, 25 right, 48 top right, 58 bottom right, 63, 72 left, 89 left

Northwest Architectural Archives, University of Minnesota Libraries, Minneapolis, MN: 60 bottom, 82 right

Maps by Map Hero—Matt Kania

AIA Guide to the Minneapolis Lake District was designed by Cathy Spengler Design, Minneapolis. Typesetting by Allan Johnson, Phoenix Type, Appleton, Minnesota. Printed by Friesens, Altona, Manitoba.